NATIONAL
GEOGRAPHIC
KiDS

HOW TO SURVIVE
IN THE AGE OF
DINOSAURS

A HANDY GUIDE TO
dodging deadly predators,
riding out mega-monsoons,
and escaping other perils
of the prehistoric

WITH PALEONTOLOGIST
DR. STEVE BRUSATTE

STEPHANIE WARREN DRIMMER

NATIONAL GEOGRAPHIC
WASHINGTON, D.C.

CONTENTS

CHAPTER 1

CAN YOU SURVIVE THE AGE OF DINOSAURS? 6

Survival FAQs	10
How to Spot a Dinosaur	12
How to Track a Dinosaur	14

CHAPTER 2

HOW TO SURVIVE THE WORLD BEFORE DINOSAURS 16

Explorer's Map of the World: The Permian	18
Deadliest Predators of the Permian	20
How to Stay Alive in the Desert	22
Can You Eat That? Big Bugs	24
Top 5 Biggest Dangers of the Permian	26
What to Do If You're Caught Near an Erupting Volcano	28
What Did Survive? These Creatures Made It Past the Permian	30

CHAPTER 3

HOW TO SURVIVE THE TRIASSIC 32

Explorer's Map of the World: The Triassic	34
Deadliest Predators of the Triassic	36
How to Sleep in a Tree	38
Can You Eat That? Gone Fishing	40
What to Do If You're Caught in a Mega-Monsoon	42
What Did Survive? These Creatures Made It Past the Triassic	44

CHAPTER 4

HOW TO SURVIVE THE JURASSIC 46

Good luck!

Explorer's Map of the World: The Jurassic 48

Deadliest Predators of the Jurassic 50

How to Train a Dinosaur 52

Can You Eat That? Jurassic Veggies 54

Prehistoric Problem: Biting Bugs 56

What to Do If You're Caught in a Sauropod Stampede 58

What Did Survive? These Creatures Made It Past the Jurassic 60

CHAPTER 6

HOW TO SURVIVE THE DINOSAUR EXTINCTION 76

The Day the Dinosaurs Died: Timeline of Disaster 78

Explorer's Map of the World: The Dinosaur Extinction 80

What to Do If You See an Asteroid Coming 82

How to Shelter in a Burrow 84

What Did Survive? These Creatures Made It Past the Dinosaur Extinction 86

We Still Live in the Age of Dinosaurs 88

CHAPTER 5

HOW TO SURVIVE THE CRETACEOUS 62

Explorer's Map of the World: The Cretaceous 64

Deadliest Predators of the Cretaceous 66

How to Walk With Giants 68

Can You Eat That? Dino Eggs 70

Prehistoric Problem: Sea Creatures 72

What to Do If a Pterosaur Attacks 74

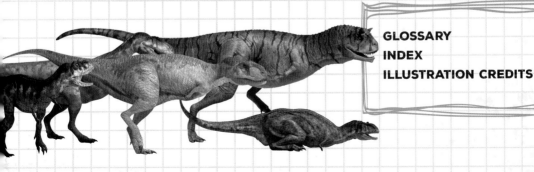

GLOSSARY 90

INDEX 92

ILLUSTRATION CREDITS 95

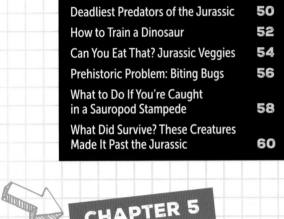

Stegosaurus

6

1

CAN YOU SURVIVE

THE AGE OF DINOSAURS?

It's hot here—much hotter than you're used to. Sweat drips down your neck. Swarms of insects hum in your ears. Peculiar plants tower all around you. There are no buildings, roads, or cities. No cars, planes, trains, or bicycles. No phones, televisions, or computers. Unfamiliar creatures are everywhere. And there are no other people in sight. You've time traveled back to planet Earth as it was between 299 and 66 million years ago.

In modern times, humans rule Earth. *Homo sapiens* live on nearly every corner of the planet. We've ventured to the tops of the tallest mountains and the bottoms of the deepest ocean trenches. **But on this strange prehistoric Earth, another kind of creature is king.**

Dicynodont

SOME ARE AS TALL AS BUILDINGS and the length of three school buses parked end to end; others are fierce hunter-scavengers with powerful jaws, jagged teeth, and sharp claws. And still others are built like tanks—complete with armor, spiked tails, or protruding horns. They're dinosaurs, and this is *their* world.

Have you ever wondered if you could have survived when dinosaurs ruled the globe? This is your chance. Warning: It won't be easy. You'll have to face down exploding volcanoes, raging wildfires, and mega-monsoons ... not to mention an asteroid the size of a small city. There will be multiple extinction events, when things get so bad that most living things on the planet die. And that's not to mention the dinosaurs you'll have to contend with, which include some of the biggest and most vicious predators to ever exist.

Of course, we don't know for certain if a human could have survived during dino-saur days. But by following the scientific evidence gathered by paleontologists (fossil experts), we can get a good idea. One thing is for sure: The world is a wild place during the age of dinosaurs, and only the strongest, smartest human could have stayed alive.

Eoraptor

DO YOU HAVE WHAT IT TAKES TO SURVIVE THE AGE OF DINOSAURS?

TIME TRAVEL BREAKDOWN

Your journey back to prehistoric times encompasses more than 230 million years, from the time just before the dinosaurs to the extinction that wiped (most of) them off the face of the planet. Scientists divide this time into different periods. **Can you make it through them all?**

THE PERMIAN
299–252 million years ago

Strange creatures inhabit the Permian period, but nearly all of them disappear in a catastrophic extinction that wipes out almost all life on Earth. Dinosaurs rise up in the aftermath.

THE TRIASSIC
252–201 million years ago

During the Triassic, the first dinosaurs evolve. They are meat-eaters that walk on two legs, varying from cat-size to pony-size. Violent weather rocks the planet during this time period.

THE JURASSIC
201–145 million years ago

During the Jurassic, dinosaurs truly take over. Lush rainforests sprout across the land, providing food for new plant-eating dinos. These, in turn, become food for powerful new predators.

THE CRETACEOUS
145–66 million years ago

This is the peak of the dinosaurs' dominance. History's most iconic dinos, from *Velociraptor* to *Triceratops* to *T. rex,* live during this period.

THE DINOSAUR EXTINCTION
66 million years ago

The reign of the dinosaurs comes to an end when a mega-size asteroid slams into the planet, causing a chain reaction of disaster so bad it turns Earth into a nightmare world for decades on end.

THE TRIASSIC, JURASSIC, AND CRETACEOUS PERIODS TOGETHER MAKE UP THE MESOZOIC ERA, ALSO KNOWN AS THE AGE OF DINOSAURS.

SURVIVAL FAQs

CAUTION, TIME TRAVELER! Prehistoric times were no picnic. Before you set off on your journey to the past, you probably have some questions about what to expect when you get there.

WHAT'S THE WEATHER LIKE?

Spoiler alert: You're going to be hot. Earth's climate during the age of dinosaurs is very different from what you're used to. There is no ice at the poles. Conditions change depending on where you are and what time period it is. During the Triassic period, for example, Earth has vast deserts, while during the Cretaceous, there are lots of lush, tropical forests.

CAN I BREATHE THE AIR?

Yes—for a while, anyway. Earth's air will change a lot during your trip to the past, with the worst conditions for breathing humans occurring in the Permian period, just before dinosaurs appeared. Then, the atmosphere was about 30 percent oxygen (today it's 21 percent). Humans can breathe up to 100 percent oxygen for a few hours, so you'll probably be OK. At the end of the Permian, though, volcanic eruptions increased the air's carbon dioxide to 2,000 parts per million—much higher than today's 400 parts per million. A human can breathe that for a short time, but nobody knows about the long-term effects.

WHAT CAN I EAT?

Do you like the taste of insects? You'll be eating a lot of those—even supersize ones (page 24). The grasses that give us grains like wheat and corn don't develop until after the age of dinosaurs has ended, so those foods are out. Depending on the time period, you'll also need to munch on possibly poisonous plants (page 41), what you can gather (page 41), and what you can steal (page 70). Finding enough food to survive will be one of your main obstacles.

WHAT ABOUT TOOLS AND WEAPONS?

You'll have to make do with primitive gear. Even if you know how to mine, melt down, and form metals into tools, you're mostly out of luck once you've time traveled back to the past. The plant matter that begins to grow during the Carboniferous period (about 359 to 299 million years ago) doesn't even begin to turn into coal until well into the age of dinosaurs, and a fire made from peat and wood probably won't get hot enough for metalworking. You'll be relying on the same items as ancient humans: pointed sticks, the sharp edges of rocks, and—if you're very handy—perhaps a bow and arrow.

DOES EVERY DINOSAUR WANT TO EAT ME?

No. Many dinosaurs, even scary-looking ones like the spike-tailed *Stegosaurus* and the enormous titanosaurs, are herbivores, or plant-eaters. You'll have to be careful to avoid being stepped on by these mega-reptiles (page 68), but they won't hunt humans. Many other dinosaurs are too small: They eat insects, lizards, small mammals, or all of the above. Here comes the bad news: Many, many predatory dinosaurs would see a human as a bite-size meal. You'll have to keep your wits about you to stay out of their jaws.

I prefer greens!

WHICH ARE THE MOST DANGEROUS CREATURES?

Each time period has its own deadly predators. In the Permian, there's the mammal relative *Inostrancevia* (page 21), faster than a human, with nasty knifelike teeth. The Jurassic has *Ornitholestes* (page 51), clawed and ferocious pack hunters. Don't forget about the non-dinosaur predators, like *Saurosuchus* (page 37)— also known as Supercroc—in the late Triassic and mega-size sea monsters, like *Tylosaurus* (page 73), in the late Cretaceous. But the most frightening of all, a Cretaceous-period beast built for killing and the largest land predator that ever lived, is the mighty *Tyrannosaurus rex*. Just hope you don't meet one face-to-face.

HOW TO

SPOT a DINOSAUR

You hear the crunch of twigs snapping. Then you hear it again. There's something moving in the forest near you—**something big.**

There are all kinds of dangers in prehistoric times, but none of them will keep you on edge like the dinosaurs that lurk in every corner of the globe. But they might not look and act exactly like the film monsters you're used to. Before you venture back in time, you'd better learn what to look for.

BEWARE! MANY DINOSAURS (PROBABLY INCLUDING T. REX) HUNT IN PACKS.

THEY'RE FEATHERED

Scientists now think that all dinosaurs probably sported feathers. Because most dinosaurs couldn't fly, some experts think they probably shook their tail feathers and waved their head crests in mating displays—just like modern birds. Other dinosaurs used their feathers to keep warm, the way mammals use hair.

Zhenyuanlong

THEY'RE COLORFUL

Fictional dinosaurs always come in shades of green and brown. But just like modern birds, prehistoric dinosaurs might have come in any shade—even neon yellow or bright pink! In 2010, scientists discovered preserved pigments in ancient dino feathers that revealed that the creatures could come in a rainbow of hues.

Spinosaurus

THEY'RE QUICK

Dinosaurs are fast, agile, and energetic—just like modern birds. And their activity doesn't stop when the sun goes down: Research suggests that large, plant-eating dinosaurs foraged for food all day and night, while smaller meat-eaters hunted only under the cover of darkness.

THEY'RE SMART

Well, not all of them. *Sarmientosaurus,* for example, was the size of two elephants but had a brain only as big as a plum! Scientists use CAT scanners to peer inside dinosaur skulls and reconstruct their brains and sense organs. They've found that many dinos had sharp senses and large brains. Some experts estimate they could have been as smart as dogs and cats.

THEY DON'T ROAR

If you think a ferocious roar will warn you of a dino attack, think again. Although modern-day scientists aren't sure exactly what these prehistoric beasts sounded like, they think dinosaurs may have growled like a crocodile (yep, crocodiles growl) or honked like a goose.

THEY LIKE TO NAP

Catch sight of a lion on the Serengeti and it's probably not running full speed in pursuit of an antelope—instead, it's more likely to be snoozing. That's because hunting is hard work, and predators need some solid shut-eye. Predatory dinosaurs like *T. rex* would have been the same way.

THEY CAN SPOT *YOU*

Movie heroes might warn you to "Keep still!" when facing down a dino, reasoning that dinosaurs sense prey by its motion. But take this advice and you'll likely end up as lunch. *T. rex,* for example, had sharp vision and an even sharper sense of smell.

Sarmientosaurus

TRACK a DINOSAUR

It's rare to find a dinosaur track in modern times. To be preserved for that long, a track has to be made on **mud** found near lakes and rivers, then dry out quickly. After that, it must be **buried** and lie undisturbed for a **few thousand years** until it **fossilizes**, or hardens. Then, it has to stay intact for millions of years more.

But in the age of dinosaurs, fresh dinosaur footprints are all around you. And knowing how to read them can clue you in to what kind of beast lurks nearby, whether it's a gentle hadrosaur or a fast-moving, sharp-eyed— and hungry—tyrannosaur.

WHEN THE FIRST FOSSILIZED DINOSAUR TRACKS WERE DISCOVERED IN NEW ENGLAND IN 1802, PEOPLE THOUGHT THEY HAD BEEN MADE BY LARGE BIRDS OR CARVED BY INDIGENOUS AMERICANS.

KEY CLUES:
- Only footprints, no handprints
- Three narrow toes
- Middle toe is the longest
- Claw marks on the end of each toe

THERE'S A THEROPOD NEARBY.
You might want to look for a hiding place. Theropods, a group that includes *T. rex* and *Velociraptor*, are fast, agile dinosaurs that move on two hind legs, leaving their clawed hands for grasping. Though some are just chicken-size, others are the height of a two-story building. And most are carnivores with sharp, slicing teeth or beaks.

KEY CLUES:
- Both footprints and handprints
- Footprints are oval-shaped
- Handprints are crescent-shaped
- No sharp claw marks

THERE'S A SAUROPOD NEARBY.
Is the ground shaking? Something big is approaching! Sauropods, a group that includes *Brachiosaurus* and *Argentinosaurus*, are all large dinosaurs—a truly impressive 70 tons (63 t) or more. But unless you get close enough to be trampled, you don't have to fear them. These long-necked, long-tailed dinos are herbivores, meaning they eat only plants. Phew!

KEY CLUES:
- Three or four wide toes in a spread position
- Handprints might be seen
- Handprints are smaller than footprints

THERE'S A ORNITHISCHIAN NEARBY.
Keep on the lookout. Ornithischians can take all kinds of forms, from the spike-thumbed *Iguanodon* to duck-billed hadrosaurs such as *Edmontosaurus*. Although some walk on four legs, others walk on two, sometimes using their hands to help them along. All ornithischians are herbivores.

KEY CLUES:
- Both handprints and footprints
- Handprints have finger marks only
- Footprints have toe marks and marks from the soles of the feet
- Handprints usually have three finger marks, but occasionally have four

THERE'S A PTEROSAUR NEARBY.
Search the sky! Pterosaurs are actually flying reptiles, not dinosaurs. But because they exist during most of the Mesozoic, you'll need to know what to look for. Some perch like sparrows, and others wade like flamingos. But some are also fearsome monsters, like *Quetzalcoatlus northropi* (page 67). Nearly the height of a giraffe, it has the wingspan of a fighter jet and an appetite for baby dinosaurs.

Welcome,
time traveler.

Meganeura, an insect that
lived during the Permian

THE PERMIAN:
299–252 million years ago

KNOWN FOR:
The most catastrophic
extinction in history

**BEST PLACE FOR
HOME BASE:**
Northern Pangaea ... but be
prepared to sweat

**YOUR MAIN
FOOD SOURCE:**
Mega-size insects

TRY TO AVOID:
Going extinct along with 90 percent
of the planet's species

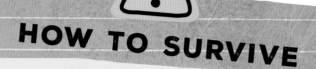

2

HOW TO SURVIVE
THE WORLD BEFORE DINOSAURS

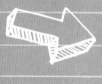

Before you can try your luck at surviving the age of dinosaurs, you have to make it through what came just before: the Permian. It's home to animals so strange they seem like fictional monsters. They dominate Earth for millions of years, until nearly all are wiped out by the biggest extinction event in the history of our planet. This catastrophe clears the world of competitors, setting the stage for dinosaurs to rise up. **Can you survive it?**

THE PERMIAN

The **HEAT** and **HUMIDITY** here are intense: Think of Miami, Florida, U.S.A., in the middle of summer ... only worse.

Take a look around:
In the Permian, nearly all land on Earth has come together in an enormous supercontinent called Pangaea. When the Permian begins, Earth is leaving an ice age, and conditions are cooler than in modern times. As time passes, the planet warms up, with parts becoming lush and green. Plants and animals—including the first large herbivores and carnivores to ever roam Earth—thrive. But extreme temperature differences across Pangaea make living in this time period tough. Be careful where you step.

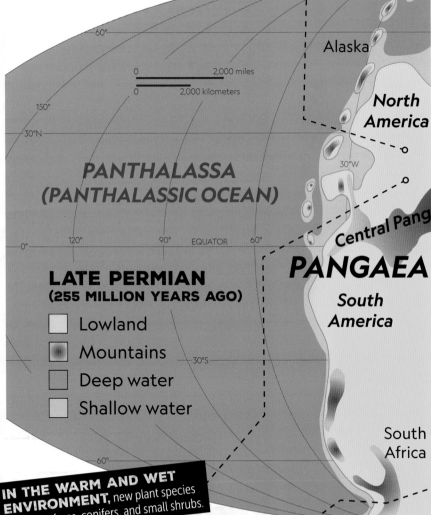

60°

0   2,000 miles
0   2,000 kilometers

150°

30°N

PANTHALASSA (PANTHALASSIC OCEAN)

120°   90°   EQUATOR   60°

0°

30°S

60°

Alaska

North America

30°W

30°W

Central Pang

PANGAEA

South America

South Africa

LATE PERMIAN
(255 MILLION YEARS AGO)

- Lowland
- Mountains
- Deep water
- Shallow water

IN THE WARM AND WET ENVIRONMENT, new plant species spring up: ferns, conifers, and small shrubs.

Southern Pangaea is **COLD** and **DRY.** Ice caps cover much of its surface.

STORM WARNING AHEAD. The dry season here is extremely hot, and the wet season brings flood-level rains.

Trilobites, animals with segmented bodies, have dominated the seas for 300 million years ... but they will soon be extinct.

Siberia

Asia

WATCH OUT! Massive volcanic eruptions occur here, ending the Permian period ... and almost every living thing on Earth.

Kazakhstania

0°

North China

Europe

ean Mountains

PALEO-TETHYS OCEAN

30°E   60°   90°   120°   150°

Dicynodont

South China

Africa

Türkiye (Turkey)

Southeast Asia

Pig-size, plant-eating dicynodonts and bear-size, predatory gorgonopsians dominate the land in the Permian.

Iran

Tibet

Malaysia

GONDWANA

TETHYS OCEAN

India

Australia

Antarctica

The inner parts of Pangaea are covered in **VAST DESERTS.** Although amphibians had once ruled the land, they can't handle the dry conditions. Reptiles evolve. They scurry and snap across all of Pangaea.

WEATHER REPORT

CONDITIONS	WATCH FOR
Progressively hotter and more humid	Volcanoes

DEADLIEST PREDATORS OF THE PERMIAN

Dinosaurs haven't evolved yet. But the world before dinosaurs is teeming with **hungry beasts** that wouldn't hesitate to attack a human. Here are some of the era's most **lethal hunters.**

ANTEOSAURUS

About the size of a modern-day polar bear, it is by far the largest predator of the Permian. *Anteosaurus* likely uses its huge skull, which is more than 2.6 feet (0.8 m) long, to knock over prey. Then, while its victim is on the ground, *Anteosaurus* finishes it off with sharp teeth. Because it's so powerful, this animal can also easily fight off smaller predators to steal their kills. This is not a creature to mess with.

FEARSOME FACTS
LENGTH: Up to 20 feet (6 m)
WEIGHT: Up to 1,300 pounds (600 kg)
EATS: Large animals such as dicynodonts

LYCAENOPS

Called "wolf face" for its similarity to the modern pack hunters, *Lycaenops* isn't a wolf at all but rather a ferocious Permian reptile. Though it isn't a large predator, this creature makes up for its small size with great speed. Although other members of its family group, synapsids, have legs that sprawl out to the side like modern lizards', the legs of *Lycaenops* are directly underneath its body, like a horse's, allowing this predator to hunt down prey fast.

FEARSOME FACTS
LENGTH: 3.3 feet (1 m)
WEIGHT: 33 pounds (15 kg)
EATS: Small animals

DIMETRODON

The strange sail it sports on its back might catch your eye initially. But *Dimetrodon*'s chompers should really get your attention first: This is one of the earliest known land creatures to have torn through flesh with serrated teeth. It also has pointed teeth for stabbing, teeth designed for gripping, backward-curved teeth for slicing through flesh, and even hidden teeth on the roof of its mouth for holding tight to struggling prey. That's one nasty bite!

FEARSOME FACTS
LENGTH: Up to 15 feet (4.6 m)
WEIGHT: Up to 550 pounds (250 kg)
EATS: Large amphibians

INOSTRANCEVIA

The gorgonopsians are the dominant predators of the late Permian, and *Inostrancevia* is the largest—and perhaps fiercest—of them all. Its two-foot (0.6-m)-long skull holds twin knifelike teeth that no other beast can match. After chasing down its prey at high speeds of perhaps more than 20 miles an hour (32 km/h), it likely uses these teeth to deliver a fatal blow to its prey—much like the saber-toothed cats that come along hundreds of millions of years later.

FEARSOME FACTS
LENGTH: 11.5 feet (3.5 m)
WEIGHT: 500 pounds (225 kg)
EATS: Large herbivores, like the armored *Scutosaurus*

PRIONOSUCHUS

You might want to stay out of the water. *Prionosuchus* is a crocodile-like animal that lurks in Permian lakes, waiting for hapless prey to come too close. Then—SNAP! Most are about six feet (2 m) long, but there is evidence that *Prionosuchus* could grow to 30 feet (9 m) long, making it twice as long as a Nile crocodile and possibly the largest amphibian that ever lived.

FEARSOME FACTS
LENGTH: Up to 30 feet (9 m)
WEIGHT: Unknown
EATS: Ocean animals

STAY ALIVE in the DESERT

You're trudging across the endless expanse of Pangaea. The sun sizzles the **dry ground. Desert** stretches as far as you can see in every direction. In the Permian, the supercontinent is so large that moist, cool air from the coasts can't reach its interior. The lush forests that covered Earth's tropical and subtropical areas during the previous period, the Carboniferous, have turned to **bone-dry deserts.**

As the landscape dries up, the water-loving amphibians that used to live here die out, leaving space for reptiles to replace them as Earth's dominant creature. But just because Dimetrodon (page 21) is comfortable here doesn't mean you will be. Here are some desert survival tips.

GO UNDERCOVER

Sun exposure is one of your biggest concerns in the desert. Use a hat or clothing to cover your head. Stay out of the sun during the hottest part of the day—10 a.m. to 5 p.m. Walk only in the cooler hours of the morning and evening. The rest of the time, make like the desert animals and rest in the shade.

RATION YOUR WATER

A person sitting in the shade on a 90°F (32°C) day for 24 hours will lose at least six quarts (5.7 L) of water. This number goes up if you're walking or hiking. Staying hydrated is key to survival in the desert. When entering a desert area, make sure to always carry more water than you think you'll need.

SAVE YOUR ENERGY

The first rule of desert survival is to move slowly. When looking for shelter or water, keep your activity as limited as possible. Don't move more than you need to, and try not to break a sweat. Rest for at least 10 minutes every hour. If you can, find shade, take off your shoes, and put up your feet.

DON'T PANIC

Staying calm is crucial. Lose track of the right direction to travel, rip a hole in your shoe, or accidentally spill half your water, and your first instinct might be to panic. If you're panicked, you might use up all your energy frantically trying to find the path, or otherwise put yourself in danger. So remember to always pause, breathe, and think before you act.

A PERSON CAN GO FOR MORE THAN THREE WEEKS WITHOUT FOOD BUT ONLY THREE TO FOUR DAYS WITHOUT WATER.

BIG BUGS

Your stomach rumbles. If you're going to last another day in the Permian, you need **food**. You glance around—nope, not a single restaurant or grocery store in sight. That's when you hear a **buzz** near your ear. The Permian is crawling with insects—some of them **mega-size.** Could you make a **meal** out of these big bugs?

During the early Permian, insects reach enormous proportions. There are dragon-flies that could do aerial combat with the largest modern birds and go head-to-head with millipedes as long as a human is tall. Never again in the history of Earth would insects be so large.

Meganeuropsis

Meet my great-great-great-great- (and many more greats!) grandpappy!

MOST PERMIAN INSECTS WERE CLOSE RELATIVES OF THE COCKROACH. YUM.

WHAT IS IT ABOUT THE ANCIENT WORLD THAT ALLOWS THESE CREATURES TO BECOME SUPERSIZE? Part of the answer is oxygen. At this time, the atmosphere contains far more oxygen than it has in the modern age—over 10 percent more. This allows Permian-era insects to fuel up more efficiently, freeing them to grow large. Then, there's the second reason: Birds haven't evolved yet. With no birds around, large, slow-moving insects have one fewer predator to worry about—and one fewer critter competing with them for meals. This also allows them to get big.

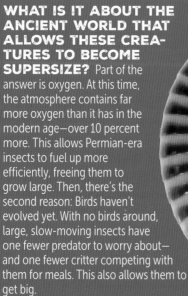

MILLIPEDES WERE ONCE AS LONG AS A HUMAN IS TALL.

Those enormous insects would have made a great food source. Most insects are rich in protein, healthy fats, iron, and calcium. In modern times, about two billion people worldwide eat insects regularly. But it takes a lot to make a meal: If you were to snack on ants in modern times—say, red ants, for example—you'd need to eat more than 30 pounds (14 kg) of them a day to get the calories you'd need to stay healthy. Even if you spent all your time hunting and eating small, modern insects, you still might not gather enough to survive.

That's not a problem in the time of giant insects. A single dragonfly-like *Meganeuropsis* would be enough to fuel you for several meals. Giant insects can even be dried and packed for eating on the go, like insect jerky. So big bugs would have been good eating.

Campylocephalus

ENORMOUS ... AND EDIBLE

△ Looking like a mega-size dragonfly. *Meganeuropsis* is an airborne predator with a wingspan nearly 2.5 feet (75 cm) across.

△ *Arthropleura* is a millipede-like creature that could have grown longer than six feet (1.8 m). It's the largest invertebrate ever known to have existed.

△ An enormous 4.6-foot (1.4-m)-long "sea scorpion." *Campylocephalus* hunts underwater but can also come on land for short periods of time.

TOP 5
BIGGEST DANGERS
OF THE PERMIAN

The Permian ends in disaster. What was once a paradise for living things becomes a nightmare world. The planet is scorched by **lava,** choked by **dust,** and pummeled by **toxic rain.** Almost nothing makes it through alive. Can you?

EXTREME VOLCANOES

About 252 million years ago, in what is now Siberia, Earth begins to rumble. Deep underground, magma—rock at such extreme temperature and pressure that it becomes a red-hot liquid—starts to force its way to the surface. Finally, it surges out through volcanoes. Enormous cracks in the ground, some miles long, spew out enough lava to cover modern-day Australia. And the eruptions don't stop for hundreds of thousands of years. Everything living in the area is wiped out.

NINE OUT OF EVERY 10 SPECIES ON THE PLANET PERISHED DURING THE PERMIAN EXTINCTION.

DEADLY DUST CLOUD

Volcanoes blast out molten lava, of course. But they also release clouds of toxic gases and dust. The dust rises into the air and is picked up by wind currents, which blow it all around the world. The sun is blocked out. With no light, forests die. With no plants to eat, vegetarians like the dicynodonts begin to die out, and then meat-eaters like the gorgonopsians do, too.

TOXIC RAIN

Things are getting even worse. Volcanic dust falls back toward Earth, mixing with water in the air and forming acid rain. As this toxic rain falls, it eats away at whatever it lands on. More and more plants shrivel up and die. Then, wildfires started by superhot lava ignite everything left to burn. The land becomes nothing more than bare dirt. With no plant life to hold it together, the ground is unstable. Entire hillsides give way in massive mudslides.

LETHAL OCEANS

As the volcanoes continue to erupt, the air fills with carbon dioxide from deep inside Earth. Much of it enters the ocean, turning the water acidic. As the levels of carbon dioxide grow toxic, fish become sleepy and die. The shells of crustaceans dissolve. And a chemical reaction pulls oxygen out of the oceans, making it impossible for anything living there to breathe. By the end of the Permian, 96 percent of sea creatures are gone.

RUNAWAY WARMING

Carbon dioxide doesn't just hit the oceans—it fills the air, too. Clouds of carbon dioxide form a blanket around the planet, holding in heat from the sun until the temperature starts to rise. (The same effect happens on Earth in modern times when burning fossil fuels release carbon dioxide, in what is known as global warming.) In the Permian, global warming lasted millions of years. Temperatures in some areas rise by as much as 18°F (10°C). The planet is roasted. Over tens of thousands of years, almost every living creature on the planet is wiped out.

YOU'RE CAUGHT NEAR AN

ERUPTING VOLCANO

THE POWERFUL VOLCANIC ERUPTIONS THAT ENDED THE PERMIAN WERE A DEATH SENTENCE FOR NEARLY EVERY LIVING THING ON PLANET EARTH. Even if animals were able to evade the lava, they faced a whole host of other problems. Dust spread through the air and blocked out the sun worldwide. Plants died. And for millions of years afterward, clouds of carbon dioxide belched out by the volcanoes caused extreme global warming that roasted the planet. Can you survive the eruptions that started it all?

THE WORD "VOLCANO" COMES FROM THE NAME OF THE ROMAN GOD OF FIRE, VULCAN.

START HERE →

IS THE VOLCANO ...

EXPLODING?

FLOWING?

CAN YOU GET TO HIGH GROUND?

YES → Go. If you can escape the pyroclastic flow, you might just make it.

NO → A volcano's greatest danger is not the lava but the pyroclastic flow, a dense cloud of extremely hot ash, toxic gas, and rock shards. Pyroclastic flows move down slopes as fast as 450 miles an hour (724 km/h). If you're caught in one, you won't survive.

CAN YOU OUTRUN THE LAVA?

YES → Congratulations! You got lucky. Now all you have to worry about is clouds of volcanic ash blocking out the sun and killing plants—the basic food source for all life. Good luck.

NO → Lava doesn't always flow slowly. It can travel at speeds of 40 miles an hour (64 km/h), a speed that no human could hope to outrun.

What Did SURVIVE?

THESE CREATURES MADE IT PAST THE PERMIAN.

Think you could endure the scorching lava, massive mudslides, wildfires, and choking air that closed out the Permian? Not many animals did. It was the most **extreme extinction event** in our planet's history, so terrible it's sometimes called the **Great Dying.**

But somehow, a few creatures managed to sneak through. When the terrible gorgonopsians and other Permian monsters disappeared, they left behind an empty planet, ready to be taken over as the Triassic dawned. And these were the creatures that did it.

My web is about to go worldwide.

SPIDERS, SCORPIONS, MILLIPEDES, CENTIPEDES, AND SOME BEETLES SURVIVED THE PERMIAN EXTINCTION.

DICYNODONT

It may not look like it, but this elephant-like creature is a long-ago relative of the mammal. Dicynodonts can grow in size to anywhere between a rat and an elephant. They dominate Earth for a time—before the age of dinosaurs, that is. The dicynodont is a member of a group of critters called therapsids, reptilian creatures that had some characteristics of mammals.

Large skull

Short neck

Walks upright, like a rhinoceros, instead of sprawling like a reptile

Turtle-like beak for munching plants

 Weighs:
9 TONS (8 t)

Size:
15 FEET (4.6 m) **LONG**
8.5 FEET (2.6 m) **TALL**

PROROTODACTYLUS

This cat-size animal, known from fossils dating to the early Triassic, is one of the earliest dinosaur relatives ever discovered. It was a member of a group called the archosaurs, which would split into two lineages in the millions of years to come. The first group would give rise to crocodiles. The second would become pterosaurs, birds, and dinosaurs.

Back legs are larger than front legs

Long, skinny legs give it speed

Walks on four legs

Small hands good for grabbing

Three parallel toes

 Weighs:
10 POUNDS (4.5 kg)

EXACT SIZE UNKNOWN,
but similar to a house cat

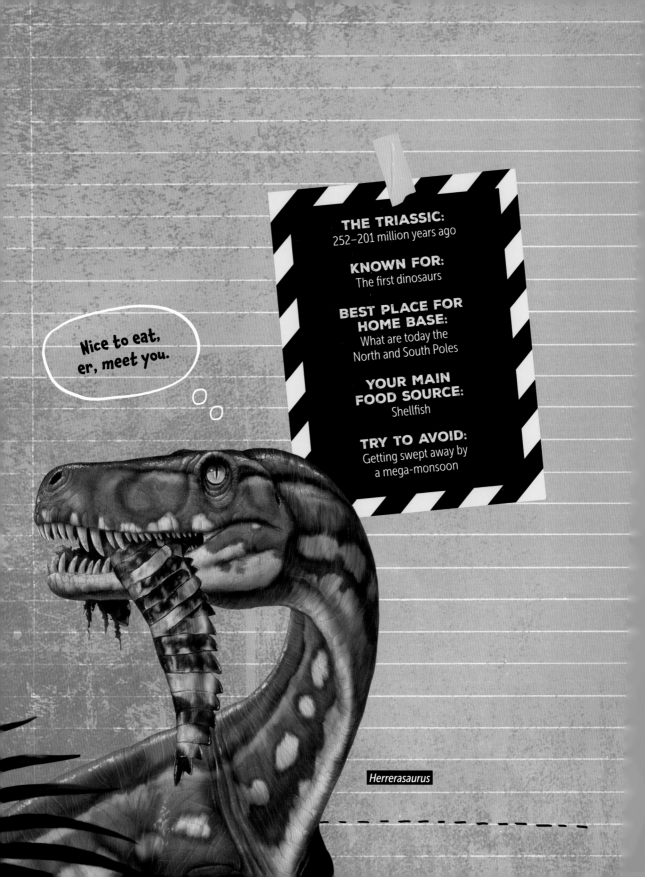

HOW TO SURVIVE

THE TRIASSIC

If you thought things were about to get easier after the death and destruction that ended the Permian period—well, you thought wrong. If you're not being roasted alive in Pangaea's vast deserts, you're in danger of being swallowed up by its frequent monster floods. Despite these extreme conditions, the first dinosaurs managed to rise up in this era. **Can you survive along with them?**

THE TRIASSIC

WARNING: IMPASSABLE MOUNTAIN RANGE HERE. Everest-size mountains are home to stormy weather and rugged terrain.

In the Triassic, Earth's continents are squashed into one enormous super-continent called Pangaea. On the one hand, this makes travel easy: You can walk all the way from the Arctic to the Antarctic without getting your feet wet. On the other hand, it makes Triassic Earth not a nice place to visit. The interior of Pangaea is blistering hot, and the land is wracked by violent storms. Choose your path wisely.

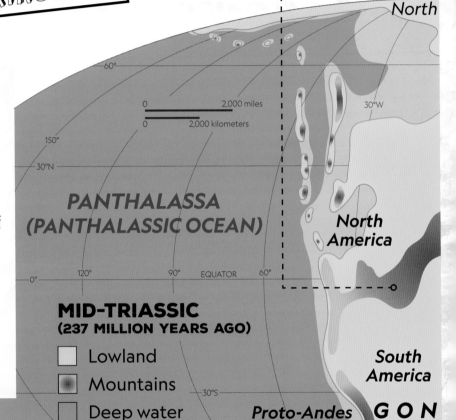

North

60°

0   2,000 miles

0   2,000 kilometers

150°

30°W

30°N

PANTHALASSA (PANTHALASSIC OCEAN)

120°   90°   EQUATOR   60°

0°

North America

MID-TRIASSIC
(237 MILLION YEARS AGO)

- Lowland
- Mountains
- Deep water
- Shallow water

30°S

South America

G O N

Proto-Andes Mountains

60°

FLOOD AREA. Huge seasonal weather shifts create mega-monsoons that cause flash flooding and extreme mudslides.

STEER CLEAR! This is the home of dinosaurs such as the large, meat-eating *Herrerasaurus* and the small, speedy *Eoraptor*.

A SINGLE SUPERCONTINENT means that Triassic animals can live anywhere—dinosaurs even roam the Arctic and Antarctic, where temperatures are similar to those of modern-day San Francisco, California, U.S.A.

DON'T GET LOST HERE. Flowering plants have yet to take hold, but Triassic Earth has forests of evergreen trees, ferns, and cycads.

Pole

Siberia

Asia

Ural Mts.

0°

Europe

North China

PALEO-TETHYS OCEAN

30°E

Türkiye (Turkey)

60°

Cimmeria

90°

South China

120°

Southeast Asia

150°

Iran

PANGAEA

Arabia

Tibet

Malaysia

Africa

TETHYS OCEAN

D W A N A

India

Australia

Antarctica

South Pole

Mollusks, sea urchins, and ammonites with coiled shells fill the seas.

Ammonite

Pangaea is dominated by **ENORMOUS DESERTS** larger than the modern Sahara. In the early Triassic, temperatures could reach 122°F (50°C) or even 140°F (60°C). Animals are scarce here—survival is too tough.

WEATHER REPORT

CONDITIONS	WATCH FOR
Hot and humid	Mega-monsoons

What's that crashing through the undergrowth? *Uh-oh.* Although the huge dinosaurs that will rule the Jurassic haven't evolved yet, that doesn't mean there's nothing to fear. The Triassic is home to some truly powerful predators: reptiles of massive size, with sharp teeth and big appetites. **Keep your guard up!**

COELOPHYSIS

The Triassic is the dawn of the dinosaurs, and *Coelophysis* is one of the first to appear. Like other early dinos, its small size means it's not at the top of the food chain. Instead, *Coelophysis* and other early meat-eaters have to use their speed and agility to hunt. These pint-size predators run on two hind legs and have hollow bones to help them move faster. They probably travel in packs and may sometimes even turn on each other for a meal.

FEARSOME FACTS
LENGTH: About 6 feet (2 m)
WEIGHT: Up to 33 pounds (15 kg)
EATS: Small vertebrates and possibly its own kind

SAUROSUCHUS

Watch out! The rulers of the Triassic world are the rauisuchians, croc-like animals that prey on early dinosaurs and mammals. And among the most ferocious is *Saurosuchus*, one of the largest carnivorous reptiles of the time. It has depth perception that allows it to see prey with precision, and large jaw muscles that give it a deadly bite. With its large size, this hunter can attack even large animals. A human should steer clear.

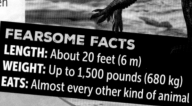

FEARSOME FACTS
LENGTH: About 20 feet (6 m)
WEIGHT: Up to 1,500 pounds (680 kg)
EATS: Almost every other kind of animal

PRESTOSUCHUS

Imagine a crocodile, only bigger and fiercer. That's *Prestosuchus,* and it terrorizes watering holes in the Triassic. Although it might look like a dinosaur, it's actually a relative of the crocodile. *Prestosuchus* has a large skull packed with vicious, serrated teeth. It likes to lie in wait for unsuspecting prey to come along, then—*SNAP!*

FEARSOME FACTS
LENGTH: 22 feet (7 m)
WEIGHT: 900 pounds (400 kg)
EATS: Large animals such as dicynodonts

SHONISAURUS

According to legend, when miners discovered the first *Shonisaurus* fossils around 1869, they used the creature's huge round vertebrae as dinner plates. One of the largest ichthyosaurs known, this colossal creature is about 50 feet (15 m) from tip to tail. Thank goodness, *Shonisaurus* most likely doesn't have teeth, so it probably sticks to soft-bodied prey like squid. *Phew.*

FEARSOME FACTS
LENGTH: About 50 feet (15 m)
WEIGHT: 30 tons (27 t)
EATS: Squid and other soft-bodied animals

THALATTOARCHON

Most of the oceangoing reptiles called ichthyosaurs have cone-shaped, pointed teeth—ideal for grabbing small prey. Not *Thalattoarchon*. This bus-size beast has large, sharp teeth with two cutting surfaces, just like other prehistoric animals known to have eaten mega-size prey. Some scientists even think it may have attacked animals its own size—or bigger. *Shudder.*

FEARSOME FACTS
LENGTH: At least 28 feet (8.5 m)
WEIGHT: Unknown
EATS: Large marine animals

SLEEP in a TREE

You wake up in the middle of the night to the strange feeling that your bed is rocking underneath you. Then you remember—you're sleeping in a tree! The rocking you feel is the wind rustling the branches you're resting in. Making your bed high off the ground might sound far from relaxing. **But it could be your best chance of survival in the Triassic.**

Most dangerous predators of the time are too large to climb into trees, and the pterosaurs are still too small to do you much harm—though *Caelestiventus*, with its five-foot (1.5-m) wingspan, would give you a good scare if it landed on your branch! You'll need to watch out for one thing, though: climbing mammals. Many mammals of the time have poisonous spurs on their hind limbs, like modern platypuses.

GATHER YOUR SUPPLIES

Prepare for safe climbing. You'll need strong rope, a harness, and climbing clips called carabiners (as well as climbing know-how). You'll also need a hammock designed for tree sleeping.

CHECK THE WEATHER

Setting up camp high in the treetops before a storm puts you in danger of being struck by lightning. The best nights for tree sleeping are calm ones. A gentle breeze might rock you to sleep, but high winds could mean you'll spend the night terrified.

FIND THE RIGHT TREE

In the present, there are all kinds of good sleeping candidates. But in the Triassic, only one kind of tree will work: an evergreen. Look for one with strong branches and no signs of dead limbs. Before you ascend, listen closely: If you hear the buzz of an insect hive, move on.

SLEEP TIGHT

Climb the tree, set up your hammock between two sturdy branches, and snuggle up. Drift off while staring up at the stars—but keep watch for poison-barbed prehistoric mammals!

IN THE LATE 1990S, A WOMAN NAMED JULIA BUTTERFLY HILL LIVED IN A CALIFORNIA REDWOOD FOR MORE THAN TWO YEARS.

CAN YOU EAT THAT?

GONE FISHING

Finding food during the Triassic is tough. The Permian extinction has wiped out tons of species, so the monster-size insects of the Permian are gone, and many other edible things haven't evolved yet. The interior of Pangaea is mostly desert, dry and barren of food. **So for your best chance of finding a meal, head to the coast.**

The oceans are devastated by the Permian extinction, their creatures destroyed by a major drop in life-giving oxygen. But that devastation means there is a lot of space for survivors to take over. And take over they do. Bivalves (clams and their relatives) make it through the Permian extinction, and with less competition for food and other resources, their populations explode. They go on to rule the Triassic oceans.

Snails, bivalves, and ammonites survived the end-Permian extinction (252 million years ago).

ALONG WITH GASTROPODS (THE FAMILY THAT INCLUDES MODERN-DAY SNAILS), these animals have the right stuff to survive the end-Permian conditions: The flat shape of these small, shallow-water dwellers helps them extract oxygen from the limited supply available.

Shellfish have been a food source for about as long as humans have been around to eat them. Bivalves are high in protein, making them a great source of energy. There's evidence that some 160,000 years ago, *Homo sapiens* lived in caves on the coast of southern Africa. The remains of prehistoric cooking fires littered with bivalve shells show what they liked to eat. There's a good chance that you could do the same 200 million years earlier.

To dig up your shellfish dinner, scout the coastline, looking for tiny holes in the mud. Those are bivalve breathing holes. When you find them, dig down. Modern clams like to hang out about eight inches (20 cm) below the surface, but it might take a little experimenting to figure out prehistoric mollusks' habits. Once you've collected some, steam them over a fire and then devour!

WARNING: KEEP AWAY! FRESH LIVERWORT CAN CAUSE AN UPSET STOMACH AND IRRITATION OF THE SKIN.

PREHISTORIC PLANTS

△ Most of the plants familiar to modern humans haven't evolved yet. So is the green stuff around you safe to eat? - - - - →

△ Ferns: Certain species of baby ferns, called fiddleheads, are considered a special treat in modern times. And because ferns carpet the Triassic forest floor, they may make a perfect prehistoric salad.

△ Moss: Many kinds of modern mosses are edible, and their Triassic ancestors may be, too. But some can give you a stomachache, or worse, they can be poisonous. It's best to avoid them.

YOU'RE CAUGHT IN A

MEGA-MONSOON

IN MODERN-DAY INDIA AND SOUTHEAST ASIA, the changing of the seasons causes shifting winds. With the winds comes pouring rain that can create severe floods, sending people fleeing as torrents of water take over their homes. Modern monsoons can be devastating. But the Triassic has monsoons on a whole different scale. Called mega-monsoons, they are so extreme they affect the entire supercontinent of Pangaea. Their waters can sweep away a herd of dinosaurs without warning. Can you survive one?

START HERE

WHERE ARE YOU?

IN THE TEMPERATE ZONE
(between 30 and 60 degrees north and south of the Equator)

IN THE DESERT

NEAR THE EQUATOR

Do you feel those raindrops? You're right in the middle of the mega-monsoon zone.

DO YOU HAVE FRESHWATER?

NO

YES

Don't risk drinking the floodwater—you'll end up with a nasty prehistoric infection. And because modern medicine won't be invented for hundreds of millions of years, you can't fight it off.

Monsoonal rains are just a trickle here, but it's lethally hot—well above 100°F (38°C). If you can find a good source of water, you might survive. Maybe.

Good work. It might not seem like you'll need water when it's pouring from the sky, but floodwater picks up nasty microbes that could make you deathly ill.

DO YOU HAVE SHELTER?

NO

YES

Sorry. With nowhere to keep safe from the rising waters, you're out of luck.

Uh-oh. Monsoons don't drive terrible rains here, but the weather is enough of a challenge: Tropical summers are horribly humid and can get as hot as 140°F (60°C). That's enough to kill a human in just 10 minutes.

Because there are no buildings here in the Triassic, your best bet is a cave somewhere on high ground. Don't take refuge in a tree: The floodwaters might not get you, but a bolt of lightning could.

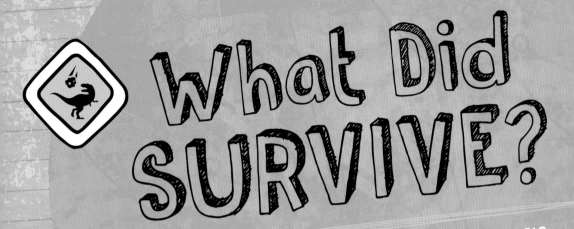

What Did SURVIVE?

THESE CREATURES MADE IT PAST THE TRIASSIC.

Things seemed hopeful at the dawn of the Triassic. After the destruction of the Permian extinction wound down, new animals appeared, among them the first dinosaurs. But the Triassic ends the same way it started—with **violent volcanic eruptions.**

The supercontinent of Pangaea has been slowly breaking apart, and when it finally cracks open, molten magma rushes to the surface, exploding out onto the land. In some areas, the lava belched out is 3,000 feet (914 m) thick! Another extinction kills about 75 percent of all species. In the aftermath, dinosaurs find a world with fewer predators and less competition. They transform from small and scrappy into the massive creatures that will rule the planet for 150 million years.

THE FIRST PTEROSAURS—WINGED REPTILES THAT WILL GO ON TO RULE THE SKIES—ALSO RISE UP AT THE END OF THE TRIASSIC.

HERRERASAURUS

This is one of the first meat-eating dinosaurs ever to walk Earth. About the size of a horse, *Herrerasaurus* can sprint on hind legs in pursuit of prey. Known for late Triassic fossils, it was an early theropod—a group of smart and fast predators. Later, the theropod family will include terrifying predators like *Velociraptor* and *T. rex*. Even later, this group will give rise to another one: birds.

Binocular vision to judge distance to prey

Runs at speeds of up to 25 miles an hour (40 km/h)

Lower jaw has large, inward-curving teeth for holding on to wiggling prey

Forelimbs with three large, curved claws for grasping

Double-hinged jaw keeps victims from getting away

Weighs:
595 POUNDS (270 kg)

Size:
13 FEET (4 m) **LONG**
3.3 FEET (1 m) **TALL**

EOZOSTRODON

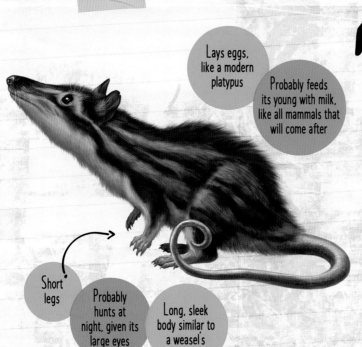

Lays eggs, like a modern platypus

Probably feeds its young with milk, like all mammals that will come after

It isn't just the first dinosaurs that evolve into being at the end of the Triassic. The earliest mammals begin to appear now, too. These first furry critters are very small—just a few inches long in most cases. They eat plants and insects, and many live in trees and come out only at night—the better to stay safe from the dinosaurs that are appearing around them.

Short legs

Probably hunts at night, given its large eyes

Long, sleek body similar to a weasel's

Size:
4 INCHES (10 cm)

Are you ready?

THE JURASSIC:
201–145 million years ago

KNOWN FOR:
The dinosaur takeover

BEST PLACE FOR
HOME BASE:
Ginkgo forests

YOUR MAIN
FOOD SOURCE:
Jurassic plants

TRY TO AVOID:
Meat-eating dinosaurs

Brachiosaurus

HOW TO SURVIVE

THE JURASSIC

Feeling proud for making it this far? Well, that was just the warm-up. In the Jurassic, Earth's land begins to split apart. Enormous cracks appear in the ground. The planet strains and shakes. Finally, Pangaea splinters. The climate changes, too: What was once hot and dry becomes warm and wet. Lush plants sprout up, a feast for some of the biggest dinosaurs that ever lived. And predators evolve, too—large and ferocious enough to take the others down. **This is a dino-eat-dino world.**

EXPLORER'S MAP OF THE WORLD

THE JURASSIC

TEMPERATE ZONES, such as most of North America and Europe, have a climate much like modern-day Miami, Florida, U.S.A. Break out your swimsuit!

DARK FOREST FOUND HERE: Ginkgos cover these areas.

What was once a single, enormous landmass is crumbling into separate continents. But it takes a long time for landmasses to separate—about the same rate as your fingernails grow. So for tens of millions of years, land connections remain between most parts of the world. This allows newly evolved dinosaur species to stomp and scurry their way to every corner of the globe. Dinosaurs now truly rule the planet—can you live alongside them?

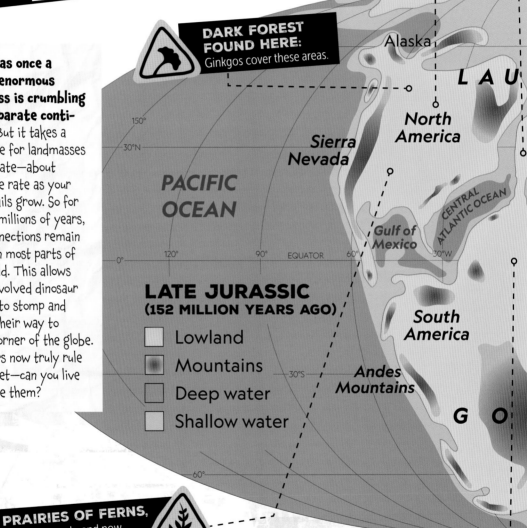

Alaska

L A U

North America

Sierra Nevada

CENTRAL ATLANTIC OCEAN

150°

30°N

PACIFIC OCEAN

Gulf of Mexico

0°   120°   90°   EQUATOR   60°   30°W

LATE JURASSIC
(152 MILLION YEARS AGO)

☐ Lowland
☐ Mountains
☐ Deep water
☐ Shallow water

South America

30°S

Andes Mountains

G O

60°

PRAIRIES OF FERNS, palmlike cycads, and now extinct bennettitales (seed plants) grow here.

LUSH RAINFORESTS sprout in the new, humid climate, covering what had been desert in dense green.

WARNING! DINOSAUR CROSSING. They use this land bridge to travel north and south between the forming continents.

DINOS such as the giant, plant-eating *Brachiosaurus* and the fearsome predator *Allosaurus* **RULE THE LAND.** The first known birds appear in the skies near the middle of the Jurassic.

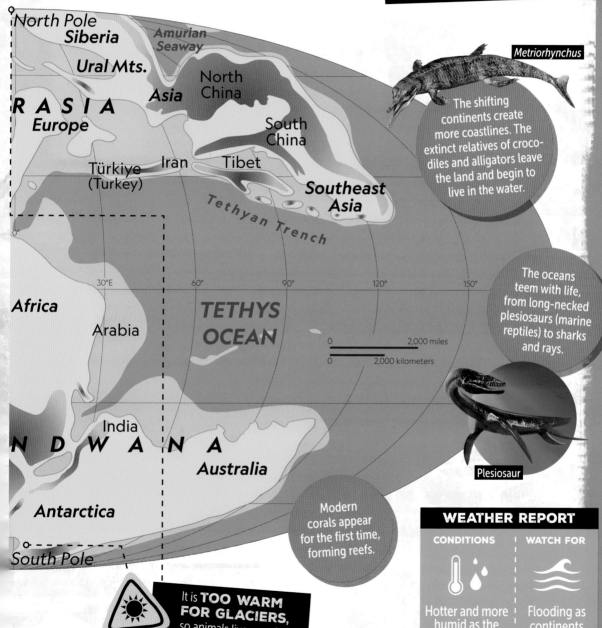

North Pole
Siberia
Amurian Seaway
Ural Mts.
North China
R A S I A
Asia
Europe
South China
Türkiye (Turkey)
Iran
Tibet
Southeast Asia
Tethyan Trench

Metriorhynchus

The shifting continents create more coastlines. The extinct relatives of crocodiles and alligators leave the land and begin to live in the water.

Africa
Arabia
30°E
60°
90°
120°
150°
TETHYS OCEAN

The oceans teem with life, from long-necked plesiosaurs (marine reptiles) to sharks and rays.

0°

0   2,000 miles
0   2,000 kilometers

India
N D W A N A
Australia

Plesiosaur

Antarctica

Modern corals appear for the first time, forming reefs.

South Pole

WEATHER REPORT

CONDITIONS	WATCH FOR
Hotter and more humid as the Jurassic passes	Flooding as continents break up

It is **TOO WARM FOR GLACIERS,** so animals live even here.

Watch out behind you! The Jurassic world is crawling with plant-eaters—which make the perfect meaty meal for anything strong, fast, and ruthless enough to take them down. And tons of **predators** fit this description. Keep your eyes peeled for these beasts of the Jurassic.

FEARSOME FACTS
LENGTH: 28 feet (8.5 m)
WEIGHT: 3 tons (2.7 t)
EATS: Large herbivores such as *Stegosaurus*

ALLOSAURUS

Allosaurus is nicknamed "the butcher" for a reason. This fierce and aggressive predator stalks floodplains and riverbanks in many parts of the Jurassic world, looking for hapless herbivores to attack. *Allosaurus* is smaller than *Tyrannosaurus rex,* but it probably runs even faster than the king of the dinos: up to an estimated 20 miles an hour (32 km/h). *Allosaurus* likely uses its skull as a hatchet, slamming its upper jaw into its victims and then tearing out tissue with its scissorlike teeth.

CERATOSAURUS

A *Ceratosaurus* swings its massive head, revealing the frightening horn on its snout. Though the horn is probably used for attracting mates instead of intimidating opponents, this is one fierce dinosaur. Weighing in at one ton (0.9 t) and measuring 25 feet (8 m) long, it's similar in size to its cousin *Allosaurus.* Unlike most carnivorous dinosaurs, its body is studded with bony plates called osteoderms that help protect it from injury.

FEARSOME FACTS
LENGTH: 25 feet (8 m)
WEIGHT: 1 ton (0.9 t)
EATS: Large herbivores such as *Stegosaurus*

ORNITHOLESTES

Like a cheetah of the Jurassic, *Ornitholestes* uses keen eyesight to spot potential prey and then its powerful speed and agility to outrun it. Its long, flexible tail helps balance it during the chase. When *Ornitholestes* is close enough to make the kill, the hunter reaches out with its long-clawed fingers, then finishes off its victim with its knifelike teeth. Most experts think it ate small animals like mammals and hatchling dinosaurs, but some think it's possible that *Ornitholestes* hunted in packs to take down bigger critters—maybe even ones the size of a time-traveling human. *Eeep.*

FEARSOME FACTS
LENGTH: 6 feet (1.8 m)
WEIGHT: 31 pounds (14 kg)
EATS: Small mammals, baby dinosaurs

FEARSOME FACTS
LENGTH: 23 feet (7 m)
WEIGHT: 1–1.7 t (0.9–1.5 t)
EATS: Big marine reptiles such as ichthyosaurs

LIOPLEURODON

Liopleurodon is a true sea monster, one of the mightiest swimming predators of all time. It uses its flippers to glide silently through the shallow seas of the late Jurassic on the hunt for its next meal. A type of marine reptile known as a pliosaur, *Liopleurodon* has jaws that take up a fifth of its body length, filled with eight-inch (20-cm) teeth. Later studies of its skull show that it probably uses a powerful sense of smell to sniff out prey from a distance.

TRAIN a DINOSAUR

Sit ... stay ... good girl! Sure, you can train your dog to perform a few simple tricks. But the idea of training a dinosaur is just plain **ridiculous**, right? Not so fast.

I got this!

Humans are able to train all kinds of animals, even formidable predators like sea lions or tigers. We're particularly good at training birds: In a practice called falconry, people teach raptors such as eagles and falcons to hunt for them. And because birds are modern-day dinosaurs, there's no reason that you couldn't use the same methods to train prehistoric dinos. Just like a domesticated raptor, a well-trained *Ornitholestes* could hunt small mammals, dinosaurs, and reptiles, and bring them back to you for dinner. This could ensure you have enough food to survive the Jurassic.

IMPRINTING

A baby dinosaur cracks through its egg and looks around its new world for the first time. What's that large creature moving nearby? It must be Mom or Dad! Many wild animals imprint on, or form a bond with, the first living thing they see, their instinct telling them this creature is most likely their protector. Usually this is a parent, but if you're in the right place at the right time, it could be you. This means a dino buddy for life!

BE THE BOSS

At more than six feet (2 m) long, *Ornitholestes* is big enough to do you serious harm. To keep yourself safe, you'll need to establish yourself as the alpha, or dominant member, of the pack. Stand up tall and hold your arms out to make yourself look bigger, speak in a loud voice, and make direct eye contact with your dino. Above all, win its respect with the power of food, giving out a treat every time the animal obeys your commands.

CLICK AWAY

When training an animal, it's essential that it understands the link between behavior and reward. Professional trainers often use a device called a clicker to do this. Start training your dino to hunt for you with a lure, an object covered with fur and baited with meat to make it look and smell like a small mammal. Toss the lure and wait for the dino to grab it. When it does—click!—use your clicker to get the animal's attention, then toss it a treat to reward it. That way, the dino will learn that it gets a tasty snack when it attacks small, furry objects.

HUNTING TIME

Training takes time. Gradually teach your dino to leave the lure alone after snagging it, rather than ripping it to shreds. Be prepared to repeat your training sessions over and over until you both get it right. Once your dinosaur reliably pins down the lure and then turns to you for a treat, it's time to swap the lure for real-life prey. With your dino friend at your side, you won't go hungry in the Jurassic.

ORNITHOLESTES MAY HAVE HAD THE ABILITY TO CAPTURE PREY WITH ITS HANDS.

JURASSIC VEGGIES

Forget a pizza ... at this point in your survival challenge, you'd do anything for a well-stocked salad bar! Unfortunately, you're stuck in the Jurassic, where **finding anything to eat—** even a measly vegetable—**is a challenge.**

The problem is that all the modern staple foods, like wheat, corn, and rice, are descendants of wild grasses. And grasses haven't evolved yet—in fact, they won't begin waving their stalks on Earth's plains for tens of millions of years more. So those familiar foods are out. You're going to have to get creative.

FORGET THE LUSH JUNGLE YOU'VE SEEN IN THE MOVIES. EXPERTS THINK MUCH OF JURASSIC-ERA DINO COUNTRY WAS DRY WITH SPARSE PLANTS.

THE PLANTS THAT LOOK MOST SIMILAR TO MODERN ONES ARE ALSO THE ONES MOST LIKELY TO MAKE GOOD EATING. The biggest trees you'll see around are conifers, ancient relatives of modern redwoods, and other plants called monkey puzzles. (Yes, that's their real name!) No one can say for sure whether these plants would have been edible in Jurassic times. But if they're like modern monkey puzzles, their seeds look a bit like large acorns and make for a nutritious meal. They can be boiled until they soften or popped over a fire like popcorn. Pass the butter! Oh wait—it doesn't exist yet.

Also keep an eye out for ginkgos, another possibly edible Jurassic plant. Hope they aren't too different from modern ginkgos, which have fanlike leaves that turn bright yellow in the fall. They produce yellow fruits similar to plums—but instead of the flesh, the large seed is edible. Roast the fruits over a fire until the flesh turns green, then eat the seed, which tastes a bit like a potato. (You'll have to imagine the sour cream on top.)

Like all plants, Jurassic vegetation has a mix of useful nutrients—proteins and carbohydrates that will help you survive—and other chemicals. Some of these could be dangerous, and there won't be labels to warn you away from toxic foods. So you'll have to use a technique that people in the wilderness relied on for thousands of years: watching the local critters. What they eat is more likely to be safe for you, too. Of course, this strategy isn't foolproof: Some foods that are safe for animals could still be toxic to you. Good luck!

Ginkgo leaves

Monkey puzzle trees

OTHER EDIBLES: JURASSIC SNACKS

△ Crayfish and mussels: Shellfish dinner, anyone? Fossils shows that both animals were abundant in Jurassic freshwaters.

△ Insects: Yep, insects are still a good food choice in the Jurassic. Look for crickets and termites—they're among the meatiest options.

△ Frogs and turtles: Head to the water's edge. Some modern-day people eat these critters, and it's likely that they would have made a good Jurassic-era meal, too.

BITING BUGS

The Jurassic was definitely a period of dino domination. But it was also an awesome time to be an insect. During the Jurassic, **insects crawl** and **buzz** around every inch of the **earth** and **skies.** And to them, you're nothing but a tasty, walking meal.

I've never tried human blood.

Because they evolved to feed on animals that no longer exist; many Jurassic insects—such as the parasite *Qiyia jurassica*—have features that would be unfamiliar to modern humans. These fly larvae have an abdomen that has been transformed into a giant sucker—perfect for devouring the blood of Jurassic salamanders. The sucker is surrounded by six spines that help the larvae stick to their slippery victim.

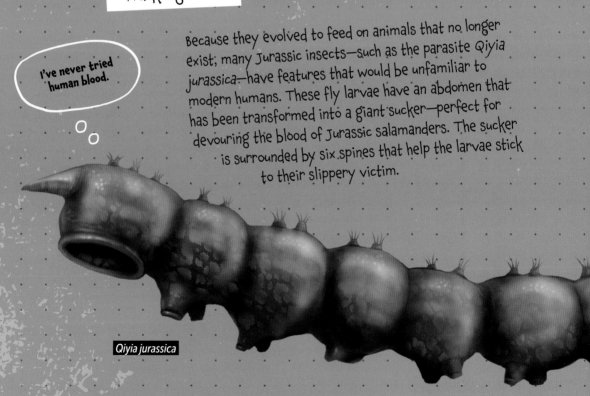
Qiyia jurassica

56

Bennettitales

PICTURE A DOG INFESTED WITH FLEAS: IT SCRATCHES AND ROLLS, TRYING TO DEAL WITH THE MADDENING ITCH.

Now imagine a *Brachiosaurus* doing the same thing! Flea-like insects first evolved during this time, and they probably plagued the dinosaurs just as badly as they do your modern-day Labrador retriever. Ten times the size of modern fleas, they had a huge proboscis (a long, sucking mouthpart) that would have felt like a hypodermic needle as it plunged into the skin. Ouch!

Fortunately, not all Jurassic insects are bloodsuckers. Creatures called kalligrammatids flap from leaf to leaf, pollinating extinct seed plants called bennettitales as they sip on their nectar, just like modern butterflies. Also like butterflies, their wings are decorated with spots that look like eyes. But kalligrammatids aren't butterflies—those won't evolve for another 40 to 85 million years.

Considering you're trying to get by in a time before insect repellent, these are some awful pests. But you have one hope: They might not see you as a victim. Modern bloodsuckers often have specialized mouthparts and attack only one kind of prey. So keep your fingers crossed—perhaps these nasty invertebrates will only attack critters they're familiar with, leaving you bite free.

Kalligrammatid

THE BONES OF SAUROPODS ARE OFTEN COVERED IN SCRAPES AND BURROWS LEFT BEHIND BY SOME KIND OF EXTRA-LARGE, TERMITE-LIKE CREATURE THAT FEASTED ON THEIR BODIES AFTER DEATH.

YOU'RE CAUGHT IN A

SAUROPOD STAMPEDE

LOOK ACROSS THE JURASSIC LANDSCAPE AND BEHOLD SOME TRULY ENORMOUS CREATURES: the sauropods. These long-necked, small-headed beasts, many the size of houses, tromp their way across every continent, including what will become Antarctica. Like modern giants of the land, such as elephants and wildebeests, sauropods travel in herds, kicking up clouds of dust with their huge feet—and some of these feet are nearly as big as full-size beds! Also like modern herd animals, sauropods could likely get spooked and decide to flee, becoming a panicked stampede of gigantic proportions. Can you avoid being squashed?

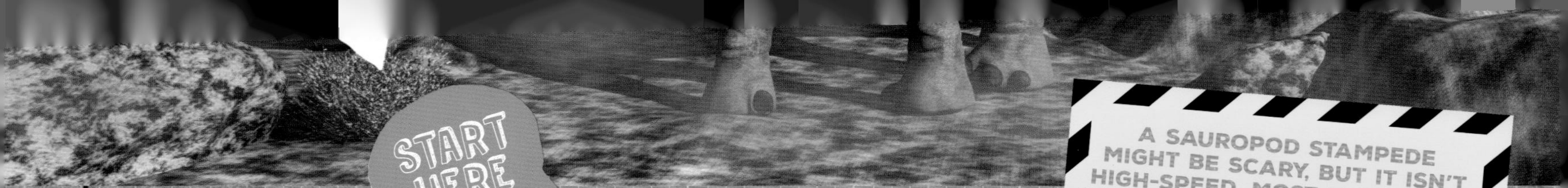

A SAUROPOD STAMPEDE MIGHT BE SCARY, BUT IT ISN'T HIGH-SPEED. MOST SAUROPODS PROBABLY MOVE NO FASTER THAN FIVE MILES AN HOUR (8 KM/H) MOST OF THE TIME.

START HERE

CAN YOU FIND COVER?

YES

NO

I FOUND A TREE.

Climb it if you can. You'll have to go high to get out of reach of the biggest sauropods, but even so it's a good place to shelter. If you can't climb, hide behind the trunk—the sauropods will most likely avoid the obstacle.

TOO LATE—I RAN!

Big mistake. Running will only make the animals more upset. Worse, the sauropods might see you as a threat and charge, like modern elephants do on occasion. Oops.

LIE DOWN.

REALLY?

Yes. Modern giants such as elephants typically will avoid stepping on a human on the ground. Of course, this method takes guts—and it's far from foolproof.

What Did SURVIVE?

THESE CREATURES MADE IT PAST THE JURASSIC.

The Jurassic period ends with, yep you guessed it ... **another extinction event.** You're getting good at surviving these! Compared to the **catastrophic extinctions** that closed out the Permian and the Triassic, scientists consider this one a minor inconvenience. Still, for about 25 million years, conditions on Earth were tough for living things.

First, the superhot Jurassic world is hit with a sudden wave of cold weather. Sea levels drop. Pangaea continues to fracture, finally forming what will become our modern continents. Where they split apart, volcanoes erupt. All together, these changes are enough to wipe out many of the long-necked sauropods and plate-backed stegosaurs. Here are two groups of dinos that made it through.

I'm a little lost ...

Velociraptor

T. REX AND VELOCIRAPTOR, STARS OF JURASSIC PARK AND JURASSIC WORLD, ACTUALLY LIVED DURING THE CRETACEOUS. OOPS!

GUANLONG

No more than about 150 pounds (68 kg), with an inflatable crest on its head, *Guanlong* isn't exactly the most intimidating of Jurassic predators. But this dinosaur is one of the earliest known tyrannosauroids to have walked planet Earth. Though it doesn't survive into the Cretaceous itself, it is the grand-daddy of the mightiest predator of that age: *Tyrannosaurus rex*.

 Weighs:
150 POUNDS (68 kg)

Size:
10 FEET (3 m) **LONG**
3 FEET (1 m) **TALL**

Crest filled with air sacs probably used for display

Jaws and teeth of a meat-eater

Long forearms

Three-fingered hands

Teeth and pelvic bones of a tyrannosaur

IGUANODON

Visit anywhere on planet Earth in the early Cretaceous and you'll spot members of the *Iguanodon* family. These large plant-eaters descend from similar Jurassic-living species, then flourish in the Cretaceous, making their way across Europe, North America, North Africa, Australia, and Asia. Animals similar to *Iguanodon* will go on to give rise to the hadrosaurs, or duck-billed dinosaurs.

Walks mostly on four legs, but sometimes on two

Beak good for shearing off plants

Ridged teeth good for grinding up plants

Large spike on its thumb, probably to fight off predators

 Weighs:
8 TONS (7 t) or possibly as much as **15 TONS** (13 t)

Size:
33 FEET (10 m) **LONG**
6.5 FEET (2 m) **TALL** at the hip

Watch out for ME!

T. rex

THE CRETACEOUS:
145–66 million years ago

KNOWN FOR:
The most iconic dinosaurs that ever lived

BEST PLACE FOR HOME BASE:
The European islands, where there are no mega-size carnivorous dinos

YOUR MAIN FOOD SOURCE:
Dinosaur eggs

TRY TO AVOID:
Becoming lunch

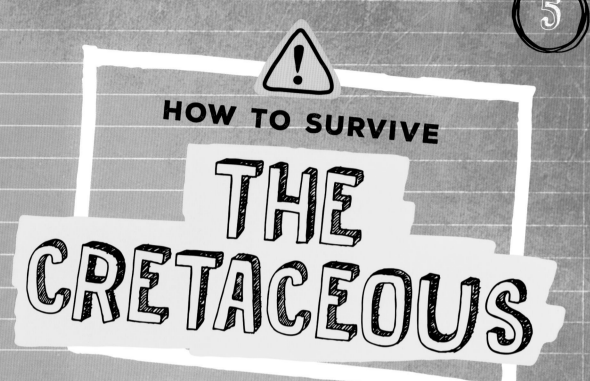

HOW TO SURVIVE
THE CRETACEOUS

It's hot, humid, and the heyday of the dinosaurs. During the Cretaceous, Pangaea has finally split apart into separate continents, and different dinos rule on each. Herds of *Triceratops* munch on newly evolved flowering plants in what is now the United States. Sauropods nearly the size of jumbo jets shake the earth in South America and Africa. And *Tyrannosaurus rex*, the most fearsome predator that ever lived, menaces North America. **Does a human stand a chance?**

EXPLORER'S MAP OF THE WORLD

THE CRETACEOUS

BEWARE: This is the domain of *Tyrannosaurus rex*. *Triceratops* graze here, too.

During the Cretaceous, Earth changes—a lot. The land finally breaks up into continents, and oceans rush in to fill the gaps. By the end of the period, planet Earth begins to resemble the one we know today. The shifting landscape makes Earth's climate cooler and wetter (though it's still much hotter than modern Earth), causing big changes in its plant and animal life. And because animals can no longer roam the entire supercontinent of Pangaea, new species of dinosaurs spring up on each continent. Some are peaceful plant-eaters, and others ... well, you'd better watch out.

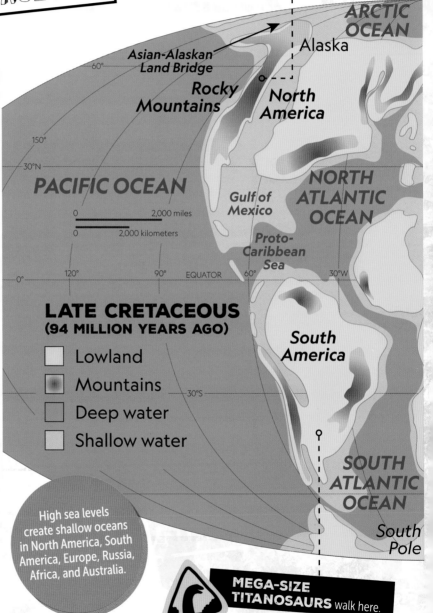

ARCTIC OCEAN

Alaska

Asian-Alaskan Land Bridge

Rocky Mountains

North America

60°

150°

30°N

PACIFIC OCEAN

0   2,000 miles

0   2,000 kilometers

Gulf of Mexico

NORTH ATLANTIC OCEAN

Proto-Caribbean Sea

0°

120°

90°

EQUATOR

60°

30°W

LATE CRETACEOUS
(94 MILLION YEARS AGO)

- Lowland
- Mountains
- Deep water
- Shallow water

30°S

South America

SOUTH ATLANTIC OCEAN

South Pole

High sea levels create shallow oceans in North America, South America, Europe, Russia, Africa, and Australia.

MEGA-SIZE TITANOSAURS walk here.

The poles are covered by **FORESTS,** not ice.

Europe is made up of islands inhabited by **DWARF DINOSAURS** about the size of cows.

North Pole

A s i a

E u r o p e

North China

South China

Earth's climate is warm and humid.

Southeast Asia

Ichthyosaur

Giant ocean reptiles such as ichthyosaurs, mosasaurs, and plesiosaurs rule the seas.

30°E

0°   Arabia   60°   90°   120°

Africa

TETHYS OCEAN

India
Madagascar

DINOSAURS use this land bridge to cross between Australia and Antarctica.

Australia

Antarctica

 TWO-LEGGED CARNIVORES called abelisaurids stalk here.

WEATHER REPORT

CONDITIONS	WATCH FOR
Warmer and more humid than today	Hot water. Tropical seas could reach 111°F (44°C).

In the Cretaceous, there's no place to hide. On every corner of the globe—and in the seas, too—plant-eaters are on the run from **hungry meat-eaters.** These are hunters so terrifying that getting a wink of sleep will be tough. Cretaceous dinosaurs include the biggest, baddest predators to ever live in the history of Earth. Let's hope you don't come face-to-face with one!

TYRANNOSAURUS REX

It's called King of the Dinosaurs for a reason! The size of a city bus, with a head nearly as long as a full-grown human, it stalks the lush forests of the Cretaceous and fears nothing. *Tyrannosaurus rex* is the largest land predator ever to live on planet Earth. It moves on strong back legs, tearing into its prey with massive jaws filled with more than 50 bone-crushing teeth. Scientists estimate it could eat 500 pounds (230 kg) of meat in a single meal.

FEARSOME FACTS
LENGTH: 42 feet (13 m) long
WEIGHT: 7–8 tons (6.3–7 t)
EATS: *Triceratops, Edmontosaurus, Ankylosaurus,* and many others

SPINOSAURUS

Tyrannosaurus rex may be the largest land-dwelling predator ever, but *Spinosaurus* is the biggest carnivorous dinosaur that ever lived, period. The first dinosaur to enter the water and start swimming, it uses a long snout full of cone-shaped teeth to gobble down fish. Because *Spinosaurus* is so big, it doesn't have to worry about predators. This makes the purpose of the seven-foot (2-m) spines on its back a mystery.

FEARSOME FACTS
LENGTH: 46–59 feet (14–18 m)
WEIGHT: 13–22 tons (12–20 t)
EATS: Fish

FEARSOME FACTS
LENGTH: 16 feet (5 m)
WEIGHT: Up to 550 pounds (250 kg)
EATS: Water-dwelling creatures and possibly small dinosaurs

ANKYLOSAURUS

OK, it isn't a predator; *Ankylosaurus* eats only plants. But beside the fact that it's covered in armored plating and topped with two rows of protective spikes, this dinosaur has one of the most lethal weapons on the late Cretaceous landscape—a tail ending in a bony club that it probably uses to swipe at the legs of attackers. The club is easily powerful enough to break the bones of most predators—making this one herbivore to stay far away from.

FEARSOME FACTS
LENGTH: 23 feet (7 m)
WEIGHT: Up to 4 tons (3.6 t)
EATS: Plants

QUETZALCOATLUS

Think of a real-life flying creature with the wingspan of an F-16 fighter plane. That's *Quetzalcoatlus northropi,* one of the largest flying animals of all time. When on land, it stands the height of a giraffe, so big it is capable of plucking baby dinos off the ground with its six-foot (2-m) jaws. Some scientists think *Quetzalcoatlus* flies like a glider, using its 35-foot (11-m) wingspan to cover around 10,000 miles (16,000 km)—nearly half the distance around the planet—nonstop.

FEARSOME FACTS
LENGTH: 31 feet (9.5 m)
WEIGHT: 4.7 tons (4.2 t)
EATS: Dinosaurs

SARCOSUCHUS

If you think modern-day crocodiles are scary, picture one as long as three cars parked end to end. Also known as Supercroc, *Sarcosuchus* is one prehistoric predator not to be messed with. This enormous hunter spends much of its time partly submerged in the water, with its eyes peeking above the surface to look for hapless dinos that wander too close. Being crushed inside its massive jaws is the equivalent of being trapped under the weight of a semitruck. Yikes!

HOW TO
WALK WITH GIANTS

How's the weather down there?

Today, Earth's largest land animal is the mighty African bush elephant, which can reach a height of 13 feet (4 m) at the shoulder and weigh more than 10 tons (9 t). **But that's nothing compared with the titanosaurs.** The largest of them all, *Patagotitan mayorum*, stood about 130 feet (40 m) from nose to tail and weighed some 70 tons (64 t). That's about the length of two trucks (with trailers) parked end to end, and the weight of nearly 10 African elephants.

Like elephants, these enormous dinosaurs are gentle giants. The largest of the sauropods, they are plant-eating herbivores whose huge bulk means they have no predators to fear. They are one of the most spectacular sights in the Cretaceous landscape. But their sheer size means you have to approach them with caution. Here are some tips for safe viewing.

68

BE PATIENT

You're off to check your favorite nesting site for tasty eggs when—uh-oh—a herd of *Dreadnoughtus* are blocking the trail. Never try to shoo dinos off your path. Instead, wait until the massive creatures move to a new spot before continuing on your way.

KEEP YOUR DISTANCE

Dinos that think you're a predator on the attack could become aggressive as they try to defend themselves. Stay far back to show that you're not a threat. If the dinosaurs start moving toward you, back away slowly.

KNOW THE WARNING SIGNS

Watch the titanosaurs for any signs that they might be uneasy or stressed by your presence. Body language to look out for might include sniffing the air in your direction, pacing or pawing, or facing you while stamping a foot. If the dinosaurs seem not to want you there, move away slowly.

NEVER RUN

Fast, jerky movements can panic the titanosaurs. And you'll want to avoid being caught in a herd of frightened, jumbo-size dinos at all costs. Keep your movements slow and steady. If you stay calm, the dinosaurs usually do, too. Happy titano-spotting!

CRETACEOUS EARTH IS HOME TO THE LARGEST LAND ANIMALS THAT HAVE EVER WALKED UPON THE PLANET: THE TITANOSAURS.

DINO EGGS

You'd give just about anything for a big breakfast, with a golden stack of pancakes, crispy bacon, and a side of perfectly fluffy scrambled eggs. Well, too bad: There are no diners in the Cretaceous. You're **out of luck** on the pancakes and bacon. But you might be able to get those **eggs** ... they just won't come from a chicken.

Protein isn't easy to get in the age of dinosaurs. You've got to hunt for your dinner, and snaring small animals, stealing prey from other critters, or spearing fish takes skill. (Also, you have to watch out for competing predators.) But dinosaur eggs are a great source of protein, and, unlike live prey, they aren't hard to catch.

Oviraptor

LARGE DINOSAURS ARRANGE THEIR EGGS IN A RING, AND THEN SIT IN THE MIDDLE. THIS KEEPS THEM FROM CRUSHING THE DELICATE SHELLS.

MAMAS (AND PAPAS) NOT TO MESS WITH

YOU MIGHT THINK TWICE ABOUT RAIDING A NEST WHEN ONE OF THESE PROTECTIVE PARENTS IS LURKING NEARBY.

ALL DINOSAURS REPRODUCE BY LAYING EGGS. In the modern day, scientists have found eggs—and also fossils of hatchlings and juvenile dinos—from many species on several continents. And for a time traveler on the Cretaceous landscape, these eggs are easy to spot. Dinosaur eggs come in a variety of vibrant colors (just like those of their modern relatives, birds, whose eggs can range from white to deep red, blue, and green). Experts think dino eggs evolved these brilliant hues as camouflage from predators: To dinosaur (or bird) eyes, white eggs would look glowing pink. Colored eggs, however, would blend into a nest. Of course, these rainbow hues stand out to your human eyes, making the eggs easy to collect.

Some dinosaur species, such as the giant, long-necked sauropods, bury their eggs and leave them behind, just like modern sea turtles. If you can find a sauropod nesting site, you'll simply have to dig up the eggs and you'll have a feast to eat.

But other species of dinosaurs aren't about to just leave their eggs unprotected. "Big Mama" is a 75-million-year-old theropod discovered curled up on her nest of eggs in Central Asia's Gobi desert. This famous fossil proves that some dinosaurs guarded their babies-to-be. And that would make raiding their nests no easy feat. Big Mama, a type of theropod called a *Citipati*, was about the size of an emu, making her a fearsome foe indeed.

△ The young of duck-billed dino *Maiasaura* were unable to walk just after hatching, meaning that their parents must have cared for them. These dinosaurs were herbivores, but they nested in enormous colonies—and a huge flock of 26-foot (8-m) dinos is likely not a place you'll want to venture.

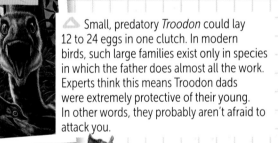

Maiasaura nest and hatchlings

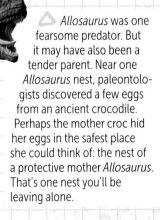

△ Small, predatory *Troodon* could lay 12 to 24 eggs in one clutch. In modern birds, such large families exist only in species in which the father does almost all the work. Experts think this means Troodon dads were extremely protective of their young. In other words, they probably aren't afraid to attack you.

△ *Allosaurus* was one fearsome predator. But it may have also been a tender parent. Near one *Allosaurus* nest, paleontologists discovered a few eggs from an ancient crocodile. Perhaps the mother croc hid her eggs in the safest place she could think of: the nest of a protective mother *Allosaurus*. That's one nest you'll be leaving alone.

SEA CREATURES

It's hot in the Cretaceous, and that blue ocean sure looks inviting. But whatever you do, **don't go in the water!** If you thought the land-dwelling dinos of the Cretaceous were scary, wait until you see what lurks **beneath the waves.** Mosasaurs and plesiosaurs (two groups of marine reptiles), as well as giant squid, turtles, and ferocious fish, are among the hungry beasts waiting down below.

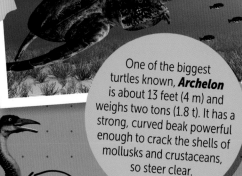

One of the biggest turtles known, **Archelon** is about 13 feet (4 m) and weighs two tons (1.8 t). It has a strong, curved beak powerful enough to crack the shells of mollusks and crustaceans, so steer clear.

It might be just a fish, but **Xiphactinus** is one of the fiercest creatures in the Cretaceous sea. This 17-foot (5-m) monster can open its jaw wide enough to swallow six-foot (2-m) prey whole. Yep, that's human-size.

The bizarre, flightless **Hesperornis** clocks in at around six feet (2 m) long and, unlike modern birds, has teeth. It uses them to hunt fish and squid, but you'll probably want to keep out of its way, too.

Globidens isn't likely to attack a human, but coming face-to-face with this 25-foot (7.6-m)-long mosasaur would still be shocking. It uses its rounded teeth to crush the shells of turtles and shellfish.

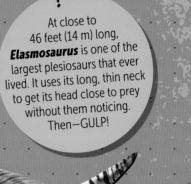

At close to 46 feet (14 m) long, **Elasmosaurus** is one of the largest plesiosaurs that ever lived. It uses its long, thin neck to get its head close to prey without them noticing. Then—GULP!

It is one of the largest mosasaurs and the deadliest hunter of the ancient ocean. **Tylosaurus** can be more than 45 feet (14 m) long, and its huge jaws are lined with multiple rows of sharp, pointy teeth. It eats fish, sharks, plesiosaurs, and other mosasaurs—and you, if you get too close.

Fifteen-foot (5-m)-long prehistoric shark **Squalicorax** attacks anything it comes across, from fish to mosasaurs to duck-billed hadrosaurs to ... you, if it gets the chance.

In modern times, humans don't have to worry about giant squid, which keep to the deep sea. But in the Cretaceous, beasts like 25-foot (7.6-m) **Tusoteuthis** roam the shallow waters where you're likely to be splashing around.

A PTEROSAUR ATTACKS

Quetzalcoatlus northropi

YOU'RE WALKING ALONG WHEN SUDDENLY, SOME-THING BLOTS OUT THE SUN. It's not a plane ... but it's the size of one. During the Cretaceous, dinosaurs may dominate the land. But for 150 million years, pterosaurs rule the skies. Some are the size of sparrows, while others, like *Quetzalcoatlus northropi*, have truly monstrous proportions. These dinosaur relatives are the first animals (not counting insects) to achieve flight. Many are predators. And some, like *Hatzegopteryx*, which lives in what will become modern-day Transylvania, probably dine on large prey, such as dinosaurs the size of small horses. Here's what to do if you find yourself under attack from one of these predators.

PTEROSAURS WALK ON ALL FOURS WITH THEIR WINGS FOLDED UP LIKE UPSIDE-DOWN UMBRELLAS.

START HERE

→

DOES THE PTEROSAUR HAVE A NEST CLOSE BY?

NO

YES

Uh-oh. This pterosaur might be hungry ... for you.
THINK FAST: DO YOU HAVE ANY FOOD HANDY?

NO

YES

RUN. If you can get to a cave or other shelter with overhead protection, you might survive. If not, you're likely to become an in-flight meal.

Your only hope is to distract the pterosaur. Catch its attention by waving your food (a small mammal is best) in the air, then throwing it away from you. With luck, the pterosaur will go after the easy meal, leaving you precious time to get away.

Like modern birds, pterosaurs can become aggressive if they think their young are in danger. Move away from the nest slowly and calmly. If the pterosaur is dive-bombing you, use whatever you can get your hands on—like a stick—to shield your vulnerable head and neck.

We've walked the planet for around 170 million years.

That's more than 500 times longer than modern humans like you have been around!

Velociraptor

THE END-CRETACEOUS EXTINCTION:
66 million years ago

KNOWN FOR:
The end of the dinosaurs

BEST PLACE FOR HOME BASE:
Siberia, as far away from the impact site as possible

YOUR MAIN FOOD SOURCE:
Whatever dying plants and animals you can scavenge

TRY TO AVOID:
Going extinct yourself

Triceratops

HOW TO SURVIVE

THE DINOSAUR EXTINCTION

By this point, you've survived shifting continents, changing climates, and massive weather events. But during this last period, you're going to encounter something truly out of this world: An asteroid the size of San Francisco, California, U.S.A., will slam into the sea off the coast of Mexico with the force of more than a billion nuclear bombs, killing about three-quarters of all living things, including the dinosaurs that ruled for so long. **Can you survive what they couldn't?**

THE DAY THE DINOSAURS DIED

THE ASTEROID IMPACT WAS SO POWERFUL THAT SCIENTISTS THINK BITS OF PLANET EARTH COULD HAVE BEEN CATAPULTED AS FAR AS SATURN'S MOON TITAN.

A WORLD-ENDING ASTEROID is on a crash course with Earth, hurtling through the sky at 40,000 miles an hour (64,000 km/h).

AT THE MOMENT OF IMPACT, there's a flash of light. Then another stronger flash. The world is completely silent.

A FEW SECONDS LATER, the ground begins to shake. The shaking grows more intense. Then, the ground starts to move like waves on a stormy day at sea. The motion grows even more violent, the equivalent of all the world's earthquakes from the past 160 years happening at the same time. Everything—from rocks to 40-foot (12-m) tyrannosaurs—is thrown into the air. Many animals die.

THEN, THE SKY BEGINS TO CHANGE COLOR. The shaking has stopped. The sky goes from blue to orange to red. It's incredibly bright.

IT BEGINS TO RAIN. But this rain isn't made up of drops of water. Instead, chunks of glass and rock have been thrown into the air from the impact site and catapulted across the planet. The rock is burning hot, and as it falls, it heats up the air until the temperature is unbearable.

FIRES BEGIN TO BREAK OUT. Trees explode into spontaneous flames, and soon whole forests are alight. It's been no more than 15 minutes since the first flash of light.

BOOM. BOOM. Finally, the sound of the impact arrives. Sound moves much slower than light; when these sonic booms rumble through the sky, they terrify everything left alive.

WHEN IMPACT DAY IS OVER, many creatures all over the world have been wiped out. But the destruction is far from finished.

TWO AND A HALF HOURS AFTER IMPACT, the winds pick up. They blow at hurricane force across the landscape. They force lakes and rivers to explode over their banks.

FOR YEARS, soot and dust float through the sky, blocking out the light of the sun. Earth grows cold and dark. On land, plants die, and so do the animals that eat them. In the sea, plankton—which also depends on the sun's light for energy—dies, and so do the animals that eat it. Acid rain falls on the devastated landscape.

FOR CENTURIES, the carbon dioxide that was thrown into the air by the blast traps heat, acting like a blanket over Earth. Global warming roasts the planet and everything that's left on it.

THE DINOSAUR EXTINCTION

The air is so hot that forests spontaneously **ERUPT INTO FLAMES.**

The world is on fire. The asteroid strike sets off a chain reaction of destruction that extends all over planet Earth. Earthquakes, wild winds, tsunamis, and rainstorms of rocks wreak havoc on the continents. No corner of Earth is safe from the devastation and destruction. And the aftereffects of the impact continue on for decades. It's a catastrophe so terrible that nothing like it has been seen on our planet since. Here's the landscape you'll have to navigate.

Alaska

North America

AR

Rocky Mountains

60°

Spain

150°

Gulf of Mexico

NORTH ATLANTIC OCEAN

30°N

Chicxulub crater impact site

PACIFIC OCEAN

120°   90°   EQUATOR   60°   30°W

CRETACEOUS-PALEOGENE EXTINCTION EVENT
(66 MILLION YEARS AGO)

South America

SOUTH ATLANTIC OCEAN

- Lowland
- Mountains
- Deep water
- Shallow water

30°S

The **ASTEROID** creates a crater more than 115 miles (185 km) across, vaporizes thousands of cubic miles of rock, and triggers huge tsunamis moving away from the impact site.

60°

Everything within about 600 miles (1,000 km) is instantly vaporized when the asteroid strikes.

VIOLENT EARTHQUAKES shake the ground.

Two-thousand-foot (610-m)-tall **TSUNAMIS** slam into the coastline.

BURNING-HOT CHUNKS OF ROCK fall from the sky.

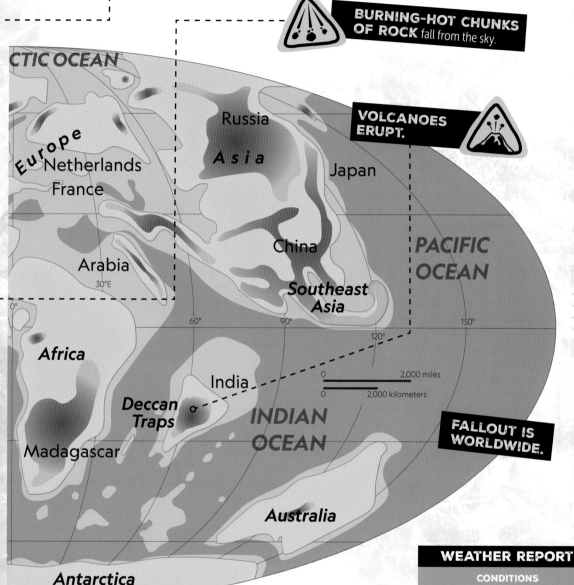

CTIC OCEAN

Europe

Netherlands
France

Russia

Asia

Japan

VOLCANOES ERUPT.

Arabia

30°E

China

PACIFIC OCEAN

Southeast Asia

0°

60°

90°

150°

Africa

120°

India

0   2,000 miles

0   2,000 kilometers

Deccan Traps

INDIAN OCEAN

FALLOUT IS WORLDWIDE.

Madagascar

Australia

Antarctica

HURRICANE-FORCE WINDS BLOW.

WEATHER REPORT

CONDITIONS

Apocalyptic! Extreme earthquakes, fires, winds, tsunamis, and volcanoes

WHAT TO DO IF ...

YOU SEE AN

ASTEROID COMING

IN MODERN TIMES, WE'RE UNLIKELY TO BE SURPRISED BY AN ASTEROID STRIKE.

Telescopes are tracking every space rock bigger than 0.6 mile (1 km) across. If one is on a collision course with Earth, scientists will know about it. But asteroids smaller than that could still destroy towns and cities. In 2013, a space rock just 59 feet (18 m) across exploded over Chelyabinsk, Russia, creating a shock wave that injured some 1,500 people. And, of course, there are no asteroid-tracking telescopes in the age of dinosaurs. The devastation caused by a prehistoric impact comes down to the size of the space rock.

MORE THAN 100 TONS (91 T) OF SPACE ROCK HIT EARTH EVERY DAY.

START HERE

HOW BIG IS THE ASTEROID?

SMALLER THAN A CAR

You're in luck. The majority of space rocks are this size, and they burn up harmlessly in the atmosphere. (When they do that, they're called meteors.)

THE SIZE OF A HOUSE

Unless you happen to be standing in just the wrong spot, you'll probably be OK. An asteroid this size would pulverize anything up to a half mile (0.8 km) from the strike site.

THE SIZE OF A 20-STORY BUILDING

An asteroid this size has the energy equivalent of a modern nuclear bomb. It would flatten everything within five miles (8 km) from the point of impact. That would be enough to destroy most major cities (if, you know, cities existed yet).

ABOUT A MILE (1.6 KM) ACROSS

This isn't good. A space rock this big would destroy everything up to 200 miles (321 km) away from ground zero. If one of these hit modern-day New York City, it would wipe out everything from Boston to Washington, D.C. It would also throw up enough dust and rock into the atmosphere to block out the sun, devastating living things around the world.

MORE THAN 10 MILES (16 KM) ACROSS

This is a world-destroyer of the size that killed the dinosaurs. No matter where you are on planet Earth when it hits, you're very likely to be wiped out—if not by the impact, then by the blast of superheated air, falling rock, wildfires, or runaway global warming that will follow. Rotten luck.

HOW TO

SHELTER in a BURROW

Getting some shut-eye during the end-Cretaceous extinction is no easy feat. You still have to find food, water, and shelter, and, at the same time, outrun **tsunamis, volcanoes, wildfires,** and **toxic rain.**

For a safe place to snooze, your best bet is to look to the mammals of the time. These small, furry critters are among the few animals to survive the extinction that did in the dinosaurs. They do it by heading to the only safe place left: underground. Here's how to make like a prehistoric mammal and hide out below the surface.

Tinimomys

MOST DINOSAURS COULDN'T DIG. BUT EVEN BURROWING MAMMALS WEREN'T SAFE FROM TROODON, WHICH USED ITS CLAWED FEET TO DIG OUT MAMMALS HIDING UNDERGROUND.

FIND THE RIGHT SPOT

Constructing a human-size underground lair is next to impossible without heavy construction equipment. Unless you can build a bulldozer out of sticks and rocks, digging your own burrow is out. Your next best bet is to hunt for a natural cave. Check the bases of cliffs to find one.

SECURE THE ENTRANCE

A hungry dino probably won't hesitate to follow you inside your newfound shelter. So you'll have to take defensive measures. Building a fire at the entrance of your cave is the best way to deter predators. Just be careful to set it at the cave entrance, so you don't accidentally fill your shelter with smoke.

DO A SAFETY CHECK

Before you head inside, check for any potential dangers. Make sure the surrounding rock structure seems sound, with no boulders that could fall on you while you're inside. Next, check for signs of wildlife, like tracks, hair or feathers, and scat (that's poop). You don't want to share your shelter with a *Velociraptor!*

KEEP WATCH

Sorry, but even once you've found the perfect cave, you still can't settle in for a long, deep slumber. A cave makes a great shelter, but it can also make a good trap. Stay alert to feed your fire and listen for the telltale footsteps of a big predator sniffing around. Hey, nobody said surviving the Cretaceous would be easy!

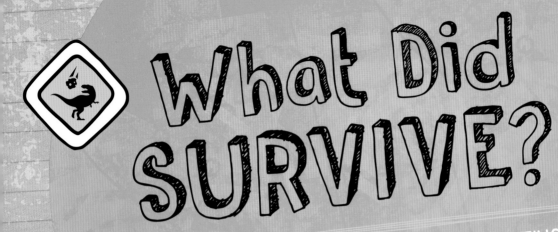

What Did SURVIVE?

THESE CREATURES MADE IT PAST THE DINOSAUR EXTINCTION.

Paleontologists have never found a single trace of dinosaur remains from after 66 million years ago. All dinosaur groups, besides birds, were **completely wiped out** in the asteroid strike and its awful aftermath. Along with them went the prehistoric sea monsters: the mosasaurs and plesiosaurs. Gone also were the pterosaurs.

Where did everybody go?

But, just as in every terrible extinction that has struck planet Earth, a few creatures survived. Here are two known to have lived in the very latest Cretaceous. They, or their direct descendants, survived the extinction that ended the age of dinosaurs.

OTHER ANIMALS TO SURVIVE THE EXTINCTION WERE SOME SPECIES OF CROCODILES, FROGS, SALAMANDERS, LIZARDS, SNAKES, TURTLES, AND BIRDS.

CIMOLESTES

The first mammals evolved from a group of mammal-like reptiles called therapsids (including *Lycaenops* [page 21] and dicynodonts [page 31]) at the end of the Triassic period. All smaller than a badger, they were burrowers, swimmers, tree climbers, gliders, and more. They lived alongside dinosaurs, eating insects and small reptiles and hiding up in trees or underground in burrows to avoid getting squashed. Little *Cimolestes* was one of these tiny, quivering critters. But its descendants would go on to evolve into modern mammals—including us.

Cimolestes is a placental mammal, named for the organ it nourishes its growing young with. Modern placental mammals vary from whales to bats to humans.

Its name translates to "bug thief" after its likely diet of insects.

May resemble a modern elephant shrew.

Its teeth have cutting surfaces a bit like modern carnivores.

Size:
MOUSE-SIZE TO **RAT-SIZE**

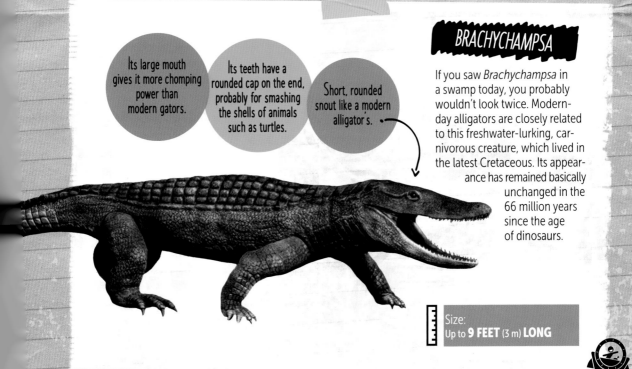

Its large mouth gives it more chomping power than modern gators.

Its teeth have a rounded cap on the end, probably for smashing the shells of animals such as turtles.

Short, rounded snout like a modern alligator's.

BRACHYCHAMPSA

If you saw *Brachychampsa* in a swamp today, you probably wouldn't look twice. Modern-day alligators are closely related to this freshwater-lurking, carnivorous creature, which lived in the latest Cretaceous. Its appearance has remained basically unchanged in the 66 million years since the age of dinosaurs.

Size:
Up to **9 FEET** (3 m) **LONG**

WE STILL LIVE IN THE AGE OF DINOSAURS

Say what?!!

WELCOME BACK, TIME TRAVELER! You've made it safely to the present. But wait—what's the creature in that tree? It moves on scaly feet, each tipped in a set of deadly sharp claws. It flaps feather-covered forelimbs. Then, it opens its mouth and emits a shrill call: *Tweet! Tweet! Tweet!*

THIS CREATURE IS AN ORDINARY BIRD, the type you might see perching on a twig or flying overhead every day. You've survived the age of dinosaurs and made it safely back to the present ... only to be greeted by another dinosaur!

Dinosaurs ruled the planet for more than a hundred million years. Then, all of them were wiped off the face of the planet in the asteroid-caused extinction that rocked the planet 66 million years ago. Well, *nearly* all of them. The avian dinosaurs, also called birds, managed to overcome the devastation. They are the only dinosaurs to live past the age of dinosaurs. More than 10,000 species of these modern-day dinos still roam Earth's skies and lands.

The oldest known bird is *Archaeopteryx,* a creature the size of a raven that lived at the very end of the Jurassic period, 150 million years ago. *Archaeopteryx* looked so different from a modern bird that if you saw it in a tree, you'd be confused. It had sharp teeth, front limbs tipped in claws, and a long, bony tail. But it also had a wishbone like a modern-day chicken and wings covered with feathers. Over time, birds evolved, losing their teeth and front limbs, their tails morphing into fanlike structures that were good for flight.

Why did birds survive what the rest of the dinosaurs couldn't? Most birds are small. The ones that survived the extinction were about the size of ducks. Small creatures reproduce faster, allowing them to adapt quickly to the new conditions. Their small size also meant they didn't need to eat much to survive—a big advantage in the scarce conditions after the asteroid impact. Birds can also eat a lot of different food sources, from seeds to insects to fish. And, of course, birds can fly. That meant they could venture far across the desolate landscape in search of food and shelter.

Those birds took over the empty planet, evolving to take endless shapes, sizes, and ways of living. Today, we have flightless, fish-eating penguins, albatrosses that can fly 10,000 miles (16,000 km) without landing, and parrots that can imitate human speech. These birds that share our planet may not have teeth and clawed front limbs, but make no mistake: They are dinosaurs all the same. And they're the true survivors of the age of dinosaurs.

Archaeopteryx fossil

THE FOSSIL REMAINS OF ARCHAEOPTERYX WERE FIRST DISCOVERED IN THE EARLY 1860S IN SOUTHERN GERMANY.

AMPHIBIANS: animals that live part of their lives in water and part on land

ASTEROID: a chunk of rock in space that orbits the sun

BURROW: a hole in the ground made by an animal for shelter

CARBON DIOXIDE: a gas that humans and animals breathe out and plants use to make food

CARBONIFEROUS: the time period occurring just before the Permian and lasting from about 359 to 299 million years ago

CARNIVORES: animals that eat only meat

CLIMATE: the average weather conditions in a place over decades

CONTINENTS: solid areas of land separated by water or other natural features

CRATER: a hole in the surface of a planet formed by an impact, as from an asteroid

CRETACEOUS: the last of the three time periods in the Mesozoic era, occurring from about 145 to 66 million years ago

CRUSTACEANS: shellfish, such as crabs, lobsters, and shrimp

DESERT: a dry place that receives little or almost no rainfall

EARTHQUAKE: shaking of the surface of Earth

EXTINCTION: the dying out of a species—or many species—from Earth

GLACIERS: large bodies of ice that move slowly across land

HERBIVORES: animals that eat only plants

HUMIDITY: the amount of water vapor in the air

JURASSIC: the second of the three time periods in the Mesozoic era, occurring from about 201 to 145 million years ago

LAVA: hot, liquid rock that flows from a volcano or deep crack in Earth

MESOZOIC: the time period occurring just after the Permian, made up of the Triassic, Jurassic, and Cretaceous periods and also known as the age of dinosaurs

MOSASAURS: large, predatory ocean-dwelling lizards that lived alongside the dinosaurs

OXYGEN: a gas breathed in by humans and animals and given off by plants

PALEONTOLOGIST: a scientist who studies fossils

PANGAEA: the supercontinent that existed on Earth around 300 million years ago

PERMIAN: the time period occurring after the Carboniferous and before the Mesozoic, lasting from about 299 to 252 million years ago

PLESIOSAURS: ocean-dwelling reptiles that lived alongside the dinosaurs

PTEROSAURS: flying reptiles that lived alongside the dinosaurs

PROTEIN: a nutrient found in food that builds and maintains tissues in the body

SAUROPODS: plant-eating dinosaurs, most with long necks, small heads, and long tails

TEMPERATE: a place with moderate weather, neither extremely cold nor extremely hot

THEROPODS: a group of mostly meat-eating dinosaurs that walked on two legs

TITANOSAURS: a group of large sauropod dinosaurs known for including the largest species of dinosaurs that ever lived

TRIASSIC: the first of three time periods in the Mesozoic era, occluding from about 252 to 201 million years ago

TSUNAMIS: large and powerful ocean waves that grow bigger as they reach shore

VOLCANO: an opening in Earth's crust that can erupt, sending hot gases and melted rock from deep inside the planet to the surface

WILDFIRE: an uncontrolled fire that burns in a forest, grassland, or some other area not densely populated by humans

INDEX

Boldface indicates illustrations.

A

Abelisaurids 65
Air
    carbon dioxide 10, 27, 28, 79, 90
    FAQs 10
    oxygen 10, 25, 27, 91
Allosaurus 49, 50, **50–51,** 71, **71**
Ammonites **35,** 40, **40**
Amphibians 19, 22, 90
Ankylosaurus 66, 67, **67**
Anteosaurus 20, **20**
Archaeopteryx 89, **89**
Archelon 72, **72**
Archosaurs 31
Argentinosaurus 15
Arthropleura 25, **25**
Asteroids
    aftereffects 79, 80–81
    crater 80, 90
    dinosaur extinction 77–79, **78–79,**
        80
    glossary 90
    survival 82–83, **82–83**
    timeline 79
Atmosphere
    asteroid impact 83
    FAQs 10
    Permian 10, 25, 27

B

Beetles 30
Bennettitales 48, **57**
Birds
    ancestors 45
    Cretaceous 72, **72**
    as dinosaurs 88–89, **88–89**
    first known 49
    survival 86
    training 52
Bivalves 40, **40,** 41
Brachiosaurus 15, **46,** 49
Brachychampsa **86–87,** 87
Breathing FAQs 10
Burrow
    glossary 90
    shelter in a burrow 84–85, **84–85**

C

Caelestiventus 38
Camplyocephalus 25, **25**
Carbon dioxide
    Cretaceous 79
    FAQs 10
    glossary 90
    Permian 27, 28
Carboniferous 11, 22, 90
Carnivores 90
Centipedes 30
Ceratosaurus **50–51,** 51
Cimolestes 87, **87**
Citipati 71
Clams 41
Climate
    Cretaceous 64, 65
    Cretaceous extinction event 79
    FAQs 10
    glossary 90
    Permian 18–19, 27
Cockroaches **24**
Coelophysis 36, **36**
Colors of dinosaurs 13
Continents 90 *see also* Pangaea
Corals 49
Crater 80, 90
Crayfish **54–55,** 55
Cretaceous 62–75
    climate 10, 64, 65
    dinosaur tracks 15, **15**
    eggs 70–71, **70–71**
    extinction of dinosaurs 76–87
    glossary 90
    introduction 9
    mammals 84–85, **84–85**
    map 64–65
    predators 11, 66–67, **66–67**
    pterosaur attack 74–75, **74–75**
    sea creatures 72–73, **72–73**
    walking with giants 68–69, **68–69**
Crocodiles 86
Crustaceans 90
Cycads 48

D

Deserts
    glossary 90
    Permian 19, 22–23, **22–23**
    survival 22–23, **22–23**
    Triassic 35
Dicynodonts **8–9**
    extinction 27
    as mammal ancestor 87
    Permian dominance 19, **19**
    as plant-eater 19
    profile 31, **31**
Dimetrodon 21, **21,** 22
Dinosaurs
    eggs 70–71, **70–71**
    facts 12–13
    how to train a dinosaur 52–53,
        52–53
    intelligence 13
    sauropod stampede 58–59, **58–59**
    sounds 13
    tracks 14–15, **14–15**
    see also Extinction of dinosaurs
Dragonflies 24
Dreadnoughtus 69, **69**
Duck-billed dinosaurs 15, 61
Dwarf dinosaurs 65

E

Earthquakes 80, 90
Edmontosaurus 15, 66
Eggs 70–71, **70–71**
Elasmosaurus 73, **73**
Elephants 58, 59, 68
Eoraptor **8–9,** 34
Eozostrodon 45, **45**
Extinction of dinosaurs 76–89
    how to shelter in a burrow 84–85,
        84–85
    map 80–81
    timeline 9, 79
    what survived 86–89, **86–89**
Extinctions
    Cretaceous 76–89
    glossary 90
    Jurassic 60
    Permian 26–28, **26–28,** 30, 40
    Triassic 44

F

Feathers 13, **13**
Ferns 41, **41,** 48
Fish 72, **72**
Food for survival
    Cretaceous eggs 70–71, **70–71**
    FAQs 10
    Jurassic plants and snacks 54–55,
        54–55
    Permian big bugs 24–25, **24–25**

Triassic seafood 40–41, **40–41**
Footprints **14–15**
Frogs 55, **55,** 86

G
Gastropods 41, **41**
Ginkgos 55, **55**
Glaciers 90
Global warming 27, 28, 79
Globidens 73, **73**
Gorgonopsians
    Permian dominance 19, 21, **21**
    Permian extinction 27
Guanlong 61, **61**

H
Hadrosaurs 15, 61
Hatzegopteryx 74
Herbivores 11, 90
Herrerasaurus **32,** 34, 45, **45**
Hesperornis 72, **72**
Hill, Julia Butterfly 38
Homo sapiens 41
Humidity 90

I
Ichthyosaurs
    Cretaceous dominance 65, **65**
    as Jurassic prey 51
    as Triassic predators 37
Iguanodon 15, 61, **61**
Imprinting 53, **53**
Inostrancevia 11, 21, **21**
Insects
    as food 10, **10–11,** 24–25, **24–25,** 55,
    55
    Jurassic biting bugs 56–57, **56–57**
    Permian big bugs 24–25, **24–25**
Intelligence of dinosaurs 13

J
Jurassic 46–61
    biting bugs 56–57, **56–57**
    extinction 60
    food 54–55, **54–55**
    glossary 90
    how to train a dinosaur 52–53, **52–53**
    introduction 9
    map 48–49
    predators 11, 50–51, **50–51**
    sauropod stampede 58–59, **58–59**

weather 49
what survived 60–61, **60–61**

K
Kalligrammatids 57

L
Lava
    glossary 90
    Permian 26, **26**
    Triassic 44
Liopleurodon 51, **51**
Lizards 86
Lycaenops **20–21,** 21, 87

M
Maiasaura 71, **71**
Mammals
    ancestors 87
    Cretaceous 84–85, **84–85**
    Triassic 38, 39, 45, **45**
Maps
    Cretaceous 64–65
    dinosaur extinction 80–81
    Jurassic 48–49
    Permian 18–19
    Triassic 34–35
Mega-monsoons 34, 35, 42–43, **42–43**
Meganeura **16**
Meganeuropsis **24,** 25
Mesozoic
    glossary 91
    introduction 9
    pterosaurs 15, **15**
Meteors 83
Metriorhynchus 49, **49**
Millipedes
    Permian big bugs 24, 25, **25**
    Permian extinction survival 30
Monkey puzzle trees 55, **55**
Mosasaurs
    extinction 86
    Globidens 73, **73**
    glossary 91
    ruling Cretaceous seas 65, 72
Mosses 41, **41**
Mussels 55

O
Ornithischians 15, **15**

Ornitholestes
    as Jurassic predator 11, 51, **51**
    profile 51, **51**
    training 52–53, **52–53**
Oviraptor 70, **70**
Oxygen
    FAQs 10
    glossary 91
    Permian 25, 27

P
Paleontologist 91
Pangaea
    breaking apart 44, 47, 48, 60, 63
    glossary 91
    Jurassic 47
    maps 18–19, 34–35
    Permian 18, 22–23, **22–23**
    Triassic 34, 44
Parasites 56
Patagotitan mayorum 68
Permian 16–31
    atmosphere 10, 25, 27
    big bugs 24–25, **24–25**
    biggest dangers 26–27, **26–27**
    climate 18–19, 27, 28
    desert survival 22–23, **22–23**
    extinction 26–28, **26–28,** 30, 40
    glossary 91
    introduction 9
    map 18–19
    predators 11, 20–21, **20–21**
    volcanoes 19, 26–29, **26–29**
    what survived 30–31, **30–31**
Plants
    Jurassic 47, 48, 54–55, **54–55**
    Triassic 41, **41**
Plesiosaurs
    Cretaceous 65, 72, 73, **73**
    Elasmosaurus 73, **73**
    extinction 86
    glossary 91
    Jurassic 49, **49**
Pliosaurs 51
Predators
    Cretaceous 66–67, **66–67**
    FAQs 11, **11**
    Jurassic 47, 50–51, **50–51**
    Permian 11, 20–21, **20–21**
    Triassic 36–37, **36–37**
Prestosuchus 37, **37**

Prionosuchus 21, **21**
Prorotodactylus 31, **31**
Protein 91
Pterosaurs
    attacks 74–75, **74–75**
    extinction 86
    glossary 91
    tracks 15, **15**
    Triassic 38, 44, **44**
Pyroclastic flow 29

Q

Qiyia jurassica 56, **56–57**
Quetzalcoatlus northropi
    as Cretaceous predator 15, 67, **67**, 74, **74**
    size 15, 67

R

Rainforests 48
Rauisuchians 37
Reptiles 19

S

Salamanders 56, 86
Sarcosuchus 67, **67**
Sarmientosaurus 13, **13**
Sauropods
    bones 57
    Cretaceous 63, 68, **68**
    eggs 71
    glossary 91
    Jurassic extinction 60
    stampedes 58–59, **58–59**
    tracks 15, **15**
Saurosuchus 11, 37
Scorpions 30, **30**
Sea creatures
    Cretaceous 65, 72–73, **72–73**
    shellfish 40–41, **40–41, 54–55**, 55
Senses 13
Shellfish 40–41, **40–41, 54–55**, 55
Shonisaurus 37, **37**
Sleeping in a tree 38–39, **38–39**
Snails 40, **40**, 41, **41**
Snakes 86, **86**
Sounds dinosaurs made 13
Spiders 30, **30**
Spinosaurus **13**, 67, **67**
Stegosaurs 60

Stegosaurus **6–7**
    as herbivore 11
    as prey 50, 51
Supercroc 11, 37
Survival
    asteroid strike 82–83, **82–83**
    deserts 22–23, **22–23**
    dinosaur extinction 76–87
    FAQs 10–11
    mega-monsoons 42–43, **42–43**
    pterosaur attack 74–75, **74–75**
    sauropod stampede 58–59, **58–59**
    shelter in a burrow 84–85, **84–85**
    sleep in a tree 38–39, **38–39**
    walking with giants 68–69, **68–69**
Synapsids 21, **21**

T

Temperate 91
Thalattoarchon 37, **37**
Therapsids 87
Theropods
    eggs 71
    glossary 91
    as smart and fast predators 45, **45**
    tracks 15, **15**
Tinimomys **84**
Titanosaurs
    domain 64
    glossary 91
    as herbivores 11
    how to walk with 68–69, **68–69**
Tools 11, **11**
Triassic 32–45
    climate 10
    glossary 91
    how to sleep in a tree 38–39, **38–39**
    introduction 9
    mammals 45, **45**
    map 34–35
    mega-monsoons 34, 35, 42–43, **42–43**
    plants 41, **41**
    predators 11, 36–37, **36–37**
    seafood 40–41, **40–41**
    volcanoes 44, **44**
    weather 34, 35, 42–43, **42–43**
    what survived 44–45, **44–45**
Triceratops
    Cretaceous 9, 63, **76**

domain 64
as prey 66
Trilobites 19, **19**
Troodon 71, **71**, 84
Tsunamis 80, 81, 91
Turtles
    Cretaceous 72, **72**
    Jurassic 55
    survival 86, **86**
Tusoteuthis 73, **73**
Tylosaurus 11, 73, **73**
Tyrannosauroids 61, **61**
Tyrannosaurus rex
    ancestors 61, **61**
    compared to *Allosaurus* 50
    as Cretaceous predator 11, **11**, 45, 60, **62**, 63, 66, **66**
    domain 64
    Jurassic Park and *Jurassic World* 60
    senses 13
    tracks 15

V

Velociraptor
    Cretaceous extinction **76**
    as Cretaceous predator 45, 60, **60**
    Jurassic Park and *Jurassic World* 60
    tracks 15
Volcanoes
    as asteroid aftereffect 81
    glossary 91
    Jurassic 60
    Permian 19, 26–29, **26–29**
    Triassic 44, **44**

W

Water needs 23
Weapons 11, **11**
Weather
    Cretaceous 65
    FAQs 10
    Jurassic 49
    Triassic 34, 35, 42–43, **42–43**
Wildfires 27, 91

X

Xiphactinus 72, **72**

Z

Zhenyuanlong **13**

For my Sloanasaurus —SWD

NATIONAL GEOGRAPHIC and Yellow Border Design are trademarks of the National Geographic Society, used under license.

Since 1888, the National Geographic Society has funded more than 14,000 research, conservation, education, and storytelling projects around the world. National Geographic Partners distributes a portion of the funds it receives from your purchase to National Geographic Society to support programs including the conservation of animals and their habitats. To learn more, visit natgeo.com/info.

For more information, visit nationalgeographic.com, call 1-877-873-6846, or write to the following address:
National Geographic Partners, LLC
1145 17th Street NW
Washington, DC 20036-4688 U.S.A.

For librarians and teachers: nationalgeographic.com/books/librarians-and-educators

More for kids from National Geographic: natgeokids.com

National Geographic Kids magazine inspires children to explore their world with fun yet educational articles on animals, science, nature, and more. Using fresh storytelling and amazing photography, *Nat Geo Kids* shows kids ages 6 to 14 the fascinating truth about the world—and why they should care. **natgeo.com/subscribe**

For rights or permissions inquiries, please contact National Geographic Books Subsidiary Rights: bookrights@natgeo.com

Designed by Amanda Larsen

The publisher would like to acknowledge the following people for making this book possible: Stephanie Warren Drimmer, author; Ariane Szu-Tu, editor; Jen Agresta, project editor; Amanda Larsen, art director; Lori Epstein, photo director; Joan Gossett, editorial production manager; Alix Inchausti, senior production editor; Molly Reid, production editor; Anne LeongSon and Gus Tello, associate designers; Michelle Harris, fact-checker.

The publisher would also like to thank Dr. Steve Brusatte for his expert review of the manuscript.

Trade paperback ISBN: 978-1-4263-7282-7
Reinforced library binding ISBN: 978-1-4263-7369-5

Printed in Hong Kong
22/PPHK/1